The
Joyful
Classroom

Practical ways to engage & challenge students **K-6**

Responsive Classroom®

ISBN: 978-1-892989-83-3
Library of Congress Control Number: 2016932288

Principal photography by Jeff Woodward; additional photographs © Alice Proujansky

Center for Responsive Schools wishes to thank the many people whose hard work and dedication to students and schools have made this book possible. Special thanks go to educators Andrew Moral, Gina Castelli, and Kristina Miller for their careful reading and feedback on the manuscript.

Center for Responsive Schools, Inc.
85 Avenue A, P.O. Box 718
Turners Falls, MA 01376-0718

800-360-6332
www.responsiveclassroom.org

Second printing 2017

CONTENTS

How Do We Make Academics Engaging?

Ms. Romano has gathered her fourth graders in a circle at the start of a science lesson.

"Today," she says, "you'll begin learning about the properties of light and shadow. Learning about light and shadow will help you better understand lots of things we'll be studying this year in science, like phases of the moon, temperature and seasons on Earth, and life—or the absence of life—on other planets.

"Today you'll be scientists. Scientists ask questions, they observe closely, and they try things out. The first step on our scientific journey is to make a list of questions. What do you already know about shadows? What do you want to know? I bet we can come up with a long list."

There's a pause as students think and then hands go up in the air. "I know that shadows get longer and shorter at different times of day," Julio says.

"Yeah, but why does that happen?" asks Suzanne.

"Suzanne, can you make that into a question for us to explore?" Ms. Romano asks.

"Hmm . . . how about 'Why do shadows change size?'" Ms. Romano writes that question on the whiteboard.

Eager student responses continue until the class has assembled a list of questions they can work with in their explorations.

Ms. Romano pairs students up and gives each pair a flashlight and an array of common objects. Their task is to experiment and try to answer the questions listed on the board—like how to make the shortest and longest shadows possible, and whether shadows have color. They can choose whether to write notes about their findings or sketch what they see.

––––––––––––––––––––

This lesson met fourth grade Next Generation Science Standards for exploring and understanding properties of waves. But just as important, students were engaged throughout the lesson. They were enthusiastic about what they were discovering, interested in sticking with it even when things didn't go quite right, proud of their achievements, and eager to learn more.

What makes lessons like this so engaging? Let's take a look.

* **Learning is active.** The students spend most of this lesson "doing"—thinking, exploring, and applying what they learned—rather than watching or listening. And that's how they learn best (and enjoy learning most).

* **Learning is interactive.** Because humans are social beings, interacting with others enhances cognitive growth. The students in Ms. Romano's class work with partners, talking through ideas, trying things out, and honing their thinking—while developing important social-emotional skills.

* **Learning is appropriately challenging.** Students can engage deeply in learning when we give them "just right" tasks—ones that build on things they already know or can do while encouraging them to reach for the next level of knowledge and skill. That's what these students do when they list what they already know about the topic and then build on that knowledge to generate questions to explore.

* **Learning is purposeful.** Like adults, children are more likely to invest themselves in a task when they know why we're asking them to do it and how it will help them accomplish something that's meaningful to them. Ms. Romano lets students know how this lesson connects to a larger

Using the Power of the Natural Learning Cycle

Generating ideas and goals

Reflecting on experiences

Actively exploring, experimenting, problem-solving

How does the deepest, most meaningful learning happen? Educational theorists such as John Dewey (1938/1963) and Jean Piaget (1923/1959) tell us that learning follows a natural three-part cycle that begins with a sense of purpose or a goal for learning. This leads to a period of exploration as the learner follows leads and interests, gathers information, and tries out new skills. Reflection follows exploration and leads to revised or new goals. When it's time to reach for more knowledge or skills, the cycle starts again.

We refer to this cycle as "natural" because it reflects what we all spontaneously do when teaching ourselves something we really want to learn. Here's how you can reproduce the learning cycle in the classroom:

➤ **Begin with meaningful goals.** Within the requirements of the curriculum, set goals that are meaningful for students and connect with their interests and needs.

➤ **Invite students to actively explore.** Limit instruction that allows students to only watch and listen. Instead, give them plenty of opportunities to *do*— to explore materials and ideas, solve problems, generate new ideas, and try again.

➤ **Help students reflect on their explorations.** What worked, what didn't, what was intriguing, what suggests a new direction for their learning? Through such questions, students incorporate new experiences into their understanding of how the world works and set new goals that will guide their continued learning.

The more you keep this cycle in mind when planning lessons, the more engaging and powerful these lessons will be, and the more sophisticated students' thinking and knowledge will become.

body of knowledge and how it can help them understand other topics they'll be studying in fourth grade.

* **Learning is connected to students' interests and strengths.** Learning matters to children when it connects in clear ways to the things they care about most—their unique challenges and enthusiasms, communities and homes, dreams and talents. Ms. Romano knows that this particular group of students especially likes opportunities to try things out and be "hands on" in their learning. She also knows that many of them prefer drawing to writing and appreciate having the option to sketch what they see.

* **Learning is designed to give students some autonomy and control.** Children given meaningful choices about what or how they learn become highly engaged, confident, and productive, able to persist at meeting challenges because they see themselves as capable students with a real stake in what they're learning. In this lesson, students get to choose which questions to explore and figure out how best to test out and answer those questions.

What's in this book?

This book offers a wealth of simple, practical, and proven strategies for building these six characteristics into lessons. One of the best things about these strategies? You needn't adopt a new curriculum or find room for additional lessons in your already crowded schedule. Instead, you can gradually fold each strategy into existing lessons to make them more engaging for students—and perhaps even more energizing for yourself.

About the Term "Parent"

Students come from homes with a variety of family structures. Students might be raised by grandparents, siblings, aunts and uncles, foster families, and other caregivers. All of these individuals are to be honored for devoting their time, attention, and love to raising children.

It's difficult to find one word that encompasses all these caregivers. In this book, for ease of reading, we use the term "parent" to represent all the caregivers involved in a child's life.

When teachers build the six characteristics of engaging academics into lessons, they help students meet rigorous learning standards in a dynamic way. Children learn content—and they also learn to love learning itself for the way it helps them grow, for what it tells them about themselves, and for what it shows them about the world. What's more, the confidence and skills they develop prepare them for life as committed, concerned, and enlightened 21st century citizens.

The *Responsive Classroom* Approach

All of the ideas and advice in this book are based on the *Responsive Classroom* approach to teaching. This research-based way of teaching provides practical strategies that raise educators' competencies in four critical domains:

➤ Offering engaging academics

➤ Building a positive community

➤ Effectively managing the classroom

➤ Matching instruction to students' developmental strengths and needs

This book focuses on the first of the four domains. But because all the domains relate to and feed each other, your efforts to make academics more engaging will have increased impact when you also pay attention to the other three domains. To learn more about *Responsive Classroom* practices in those domains, see the Further Resources list on page 197.

A word about who's speaking

Lynn Bechtel and Kristen Vincent—who together have extensive experience in classrooms at all levels—crafted this book, and have drawn on their experiences as teachers and teacher educators for many of the examples and practical suggestions. The "I" voice speaks for both of them.

WORKS CITED

Dewey, J. (1938/1963). *Experience and Education.* New York: Collier MacMillan.

Piaget, J. (1923/1959). *The Language and Thought of the Child.* New York: Humanities Press.

Getting to Know Your Students

On a bright November morning, Mr. Hogarth stands at the door of the third grade classroom to greet students as they enter. "Hey Marcus," he says, "how's that new puppy?" "Shayla! Good to see you. Is your grandma still visiting?" "Good morning, Maurice. We're going to read a story about trains today. You psyched?"

It's apparent from his greetings that he has gotten to know these students well. Before the school year started, he checked in with the second grade teachers and the school counselor and nurse to learn about the children's strengths and challenges. And he invited parents and children to stop by on the days when he was organizing the classroom so he could begin getting to know them in an informal setting.

As the school year got under way, Mr. Hogarth observed the students at work and at play. He paid attention to what they talked about, how each learned, where each one excelled and struggled, how they connected with their peers and with adults, what turned them off and what excited them. Now he draws on this knowledge to plan lessons that reach out to the learner in each child. And throughout the year, his efforts to know these students will continue so that he stays in tune with them as they grow and develop. These ongoing observations and adjustments are critical if Mr. Hogarth is to ensure that the learning in this class will be engaging to all students.

Sometimes, in the midst of our busy days and our need to meet curriculum goals, we lose sight of a fundamental fact: To create academically engaging classrooms, we need to know our students—as a group and as individuals. Although not every child will love every lesson we plan, we want to make sure that something in each lesson speaks to each child. How can we get to know students as learners and as people—to discover their learning needs, aptitudes, and interests? In this chapter, we offer four key things you can do:

* Talk with students about their hopes and dreams for the year

* Actively observe students

* Invite students to share information about their lives outside of school

* Connect with parents

Talk With Students About Their Hopes and Dreams for the Year

Each year during the first week of school, I asked students to reflect on what they'd found enjoyable and challenging the year before. Then I gave them an overview of the learning I'd planned. Finally, working from that overview, we brainstormed individual learning goals—or hopes and dreams—for the coming year.

Responses were as varied as the students themselves. Some named social goals ("I want to make a new friend"); some focused on academics ("I hope we do more experiments"). In every case, I felt that by listening to their hopes and dreams I'd taken an important step toward getting to know the students.

Inviting students to answer the important question "What do you hope to do and learn this school year?" can give you insight into where students' passions lie and how they understand themselves as learners. You might learn that Lucius is a budding writer when he says "I want to write more stories" and that Janelle has an interest in mathematics when she announces "I hope to learn how to multiply and divide fractions."

Students may also share challenges they see themselves facing. Martine wants to memorize addition facts this year—which might prompt you to wonder if addition facts are an area of concern for her. When Joseph says he'd like to read longer chapter books, you might make a mental note to check the classroom library for chapter books at his reading level on topics that might interest him.

Asking students to share their hopes and dreams for the school year also communicates that what they care about matters at school and that they can have a say in what they'll learn. This message can help set the tone for collaboration and respect.

Actively Observe Students

On some level, we're always observing the students we teach. As we interact with them one on one and in groups, lead discussions, facilitate activities, and referee games, a part of our mind is registering their behaviors, enthusiasms, and aptitudes and storing that information away.

But by making observation intentional and taking time each day to actively observe children, we can learn a lot more about who they are as a group and as individuals. We can then use that knowledge to inform daily classroom planning and heighten students' engagement with their learning.

Sometimes you'll observe the entire class, and sometimes you'll sit with one or a few students, at a table or on the floor. Whatever your vantage point, make notes as you observe and interact with students. Then try to take a few minutes at the end of the school day, while the information is still fresh in your mind, to review and reflect on your observations.

What to look for

Here are some questions to guide your observations:

 ✳ **Peer relationships:** Who sits with whom? Who plays together during recess? Who leads and who follows? Knowing how children usually interact helps you structure working groups and collaborative projects that stretch as well as support each student.

* **Physical activity:** Who has a lot of energy to burn? Who prefers to sit quietly and read? Who participates, and who sits back? With a sense of children's typical energy levels, you can plan a range of learning experiences and incorporate appropriate amounts of movement into daily classroom life.

* **Mental energy:** Which students persevere even when things get a bit tricky? Which tire quickly, lose focus frequently, or get easily frustrated? As you gauge children's mental energy, you'll be able to plan regular check-ins for some, longer periods of independent work for others, and strategies for those who need help sustaining attention during challenging tasks.

F A Q • What about using formal assessments?

There are many summative and formative assessments, inventories, and checklists that can help you learn about students' academic skills and learning styles. These routes to knowing students can be quite useful and are very much a part of most teachers' practice. However, our focus in this book is on less formal ways of knowing children that can be integrated into daily life in the classroom.

---

* **Learning styles:** Do some students prefer to use pictures to understand concepts? Do others learn better from verbal or written explanations? Which ones like to use their hands to manipulate things and their bodies to act out ideas? The better you know students' learning styles, the more you can design lessons with activities and choices that use their dominant style—and strengthen their less developed styles.

* **Language and cognitive skills:** How well do students express ideas in words, understand what others say, paraphrase, and grasp metaphors? What about their logic, reasoning, and synthesizing abilities? How quickly do they process information and perform complex tasks? Knowing where students stand with these skills helps you craft lessons that play to their strengths and also offer them appropriate risks.

A second grade teacher observes and learns as children share

To get an idea of how active observation can help you learn about one key skill set—students' listening and speaking skills—let's listen in on a second grade class gathered one morning in a circle.

After a lively greeting, Ms. DuBois announces that to jump-start a unit on animals and their habitats, students will share one at a time around the circle about an animal they like a lot.

Ms. DuBois models the sharing, saying, "An animal I like a lot is the snake. I like snakes because they don't have any legs, yet they travel really fast!" She then gives students some time to think of what they want to share.

Andrea begins the sharing. "An animal I like a lot is tree frogs. We've got them in our yard, and I love the way they chirp at each other."

William is next. "We just got a new puppy," he says. He pauses a moment before adding, "I like it." He turns expectantly to the student next to him, Maria.

Maria, fiddling with her shoelace, doesn't say anything. "Maria?" Ms. DuBois prompts. "Do you have an animal you like a lot?"

"Oh, yeah," Maria says without looking up. "I like spiders. They make huge webs in our backyard."

The sharing continues around the circle. Each child has something to share, although some, like Maria, need prompting. At the end of the sharing, everyone has learned something about their classmates—who has a new pet, likes spiders, or thinks frogs are neat. And Ms. DuBois has learned a lot about their skills.

She noticed that some students spoke up clearly and loudly and others spoke so softly they needed to repeat their sharing. A few stared at the floor while they spoke. Several were quick with ideas; several others seemed hesitant. She also saw that some students had the self-control to sit quietly throughout the sharing and some fidgeted. Most nodded and seemed to be listening; one or two looked as if their minds were miles away.

By carefully observing this simple sharing, Ms. DuBois has gathered important information about students' lives as well as their skills—information she'll use to plan lessons that will engage their interest, help with their challenges, and build on their strengths.

Use structured academic activities as opportunities to observe and learn

Academic-based lesson openers, warm-ups, brain breaks, energizers—all are golden opportunities to learn what students do and do not know, how they process information, and how adept they are with social-emotional skills such as sharing, following directions, cooperating, and practicing self-control.

These activities are especially useful for getting to know students at the start of the year, but using them throughout the year lets you see how students are changing as their comfort with you and each other grows and their skills develop.

For example, one year I had a fourth grade class that loved doing the Human Protractor activity, in which everyone starts by touching their toes and then gradually straightens up, arms out in front of them, as the leader calls out a range of degrees from 1 to 180—1 degree, 15 degrees, 45 degrees, etc. When the leader calls out "180 degrees," students' hands are reaching overhead.

After the first round, I'd call out the same degree numbers but this time in random order. For more of a challenge, I'd give equations and students would take the position that represented the answer.

One day, as I watched the class do this activity, I noticed that Joanie quickly figured out the answer to the equation and confidently took the correct position. This was new for Joanie. Earlier in the year, she would have been much more hesitant, checking in with other students to see if she'd got it right.

My observation told me that the work Joanie had been doing to learn her math facts had paid off. I also learned that she'd gained social confidence. I then planned ways to build on those strengths in upcoming lessons and activities.

Here are some other structured activities to try:

Matching Cards (grades K–6). Useful for any subject area or topic, this activity will help you learn which students might need more practice with certain concepts and which might be ready for more challenging work.

Pass out premade cards. Tell students what they will do after they find their match; for example, you might want them to sit down with their partner in the circle or find a spot in the classroom to get started on some work.

Students then mix and mingle, looking for classmates with matching cards. Some ideas for matching cards:

* *Numerals:* Younger grades can match single numbers; older students can find groups of numbers that equal 10 or 20 or 100. Half the students could have numeral cards; the other half could have pictures of items or dots to represent the value of the numerals.

* *Math facts:* Half the students have the number equation and half have the solution.

* *Math word problems:* Half the students have a word problem and half have the equation and the solution.

* *Money:* Students with number cards look for a card showing a combination of coins that equals the number on their card.

* *Fractions:* Students look for an equivalent fraction to the one on their card.

* *Rhyming:* Students match words that rhyme.

* *Letters:* Students match lower- and upper-case letters.

* *Vocabulary:* Students match vocabulary words and their definitions.

To set all students up for success, make sure to include various levels of challenge in each set of cards, and if necessary, choose who gets which card.

ReACT! (grades 1–3). With this drama activity, you can quickly check students' comprehension and understanding of character traits. You'll also gain insight into students' abilities to understand the feelings and actions of others.

Students find a spot in the classroom where they'll have space to move safely. Tell them they'll be "stepping into the shoes" of a character from a recent read-aloud. For example, if you've recently read *Brave Irene* by William Steig, students will "become" Irene for the remainder of this activity.

Read a short section of the text. Then ask, "How would Irene react?" Students may use facial expressions, physical movement, or sounds to show their answer.

Signal students to return to a neutral body and face. Repeat for two or three more sections of the book.

Scrambled Sentence (grades 4–6). Use this activity to see which students can successfully apply editing and revising strategies. You can also note which students are taking risks by offering ideas to the reviser.

Explain that the goal of this activity is to revise a sentence for clarity. Display a pocket chart in which you've placed words and punctuation out of order. For example, the pocket chart might read "not car. The red but win fast, fast race drove to enough."

Ask for a volunteer to be the reviser—the person who asks for student suggestions and moves the cards around accordingly. For example, a student might say, "Put 'The' at the start of the sentence." The reviser follows the command and asks for another. When the class believes they have the sentence revised correctly, they signal with a thumbs-up or crossed arms. Then reveal the sentence in its correct form on a chart or whiteboard and invite students to compare and contrast the two sentences.

Invite Students to Share About Their Lives

Of course, what you see of students during the school day is just a piece of the puzzle—their lives outside of school play a large role in shaping who they are and often influence how they think about school. In the opening vignette, Mr. Hogarth's friendly greetings for each student were informed by his knowledge of their lives—who had a new puppy, whose grandmother was visiting, who loved trains. Knowing as much as you can about students' lives outside of school is an important part of building positive relationships with them.

One way to learn about children's lives is to structure opportunities for them to share information with you and their classmates. You'll get to know them better as people, and you'll also learn important information about social-emotional skills such as their ability to maintain self-control, wait their turn, and respond respectfully. Additionally, this personal sharing helps build a positive classroom community and a sense of empathy and respect among peers.

Students can share about their personal lives at any point during the day, but this kind of sharing is an especially great way to begin or end the day. You could gather children for a few minutes in the morning before lessons begin or you might incorporate personal sharing into a closing circle.

After naming the topic, you can:

 * Have each student briefly share one bit of information

 * Have one or two students share for a few minutes and then invite classmates' questions and comments about the sharing

 * Have students share with partners while you circulate and listen

Some ideas for sharing topics:

 * Favorites (food, animal, day of the week, sport, season)

 * Weekend plans

 * A treasured memory

 * Special interests and skills

 * A language other than English that students speak or want to learn

 * Family traditions, family members, and pets

To ensure success with sharing, start small and build slowly, modeling key skills as needed. For example, early in the year, structure around-the-circle sharing with clear directions and a focused topic, such as one thing students enjoy doing after school. When students are comfortable with this form of sharing, they can practice sharing information with a partner—again, give them a focused topic to help them stay on track.

As students build their sharing skills, you might begin having a few share information with the entire class. Remember to model key skills as you introduce each new sharing format.

Connect With Parents

Parents are experts on their own children—what energizes and delights them, what they do when they stumble, how they show they are upset, and what comforts them when they are worried. That's why connecting with parents early and often is key to learning as much as you can about students.

Sample letter to families

Welcome!

As a part of our back-to-school tradition, we hold family conferences early in the year. This conference will help me begin to know you and your child and give you a chance to ask questions about the coming year.

Here are some of the things we might talk about:

• What are your child's strengths? Challenges?

• What do you think is most important for your child to learn this year?

• What does your child like about school? Dislike about school?

• What was something that your child really enjoyed about his/her class last year?

• What responsibilities does your child have at home?

• Where and when does your child do his/her homework (including reading)? How did homework work out last year (too hard, easy, needed help)?

• What are some questions you have for me?

I look forward to our home-school partnership this year!

Sincerely,
Ms. Smith

Try to start the school year by inviting parents to share about their child with you. You can mail a letter home, send an email, or make a phone call. Each August, I sent a letter to parents introducing myself and letting everyone know I was excited to meet them and begin the school year. Some teachers send home a questionnaire or interview sheet for parents to complete. This might include questions such as:

✳ How does your child learn best?

✳ What are your child's interests?

✳ What are your child's strengths? What do they need help with?

You could also invite parents to share their own goals for their child, asking questions such as "What do you think is most important for your child to learn this year?" or "What's your biggest hope for your child this year?" Questions like these provide important insights and set a tone of collaboration from day one. Then, be sure to keep the communication channels open with regular contact throughout the year.

You can also invite parents into the classroom. For example, at various times of the year you can ask a family to come into the classroom to share a short presentation about their family traditions. This sharing could connect to your curriculum or focus on a holiday. One family might talk about their tradition of having extended family reunions every five years; another might show pictures of how they celebrate the new year; yet another might share a favorite Friday night activity.

Classroom Snapshot

Primary grade teacher Shiala Higgs celebrated a "Special Day" for each child in her class. She planned these around families' schedules so that they could participate in their child's Special Day.

The night before a child's Special Day she sent home a "magic suitcase" that families filled with items depicting their traditions and interests.

On the Special Day, family members and the child shared the contents of the suitcase with the class, focusing on what made their family special.

FINAL THOUGHT: LOOK FOR THE GLIMMERS OF GOLD

Taking the time to get to know students will yield rich rewards. Throughout this book, the strategies you'll learn about draw on your knowledge and understanding of the children you teach. We encourage you to take as many opportunities as you can to listen, to watch, and to engage with children so that you can get to know them in all their rich diversity—their learning styles, strengths and struggles, turn-offs and passions—everything that makes each child shine. Finding those glimmers of gold will help you create learning environments that engage and nurture all the children you teach.

Partnering and Grouping Students for Collaborative Learning

On a chilly February day, Ms. Forsyth's first grade class is beginning a poetry unit. The focus for today's lesson is how poets carefully choose words to create a mental image for the reader. She connects this assignment to their science lessons about the five senses, and to the descriptive poem they read together earlier during their morning gathering.

Ms. Forsyth assigns partners and gives each pair a picture that has a colorful and detailed nature scene. The partners' job is to brainstorm words that a poet might use to convey this picture to readers. They dig into their task.

As students work, Ms. Forsyth moves around the room, listening to conversations and answering questions. She pauses by Primiti and Caitlin, who are looking intently at a photograph of a stream running through woods.

"I bet it smells wet there," Primiti says.

"Yes!" Caitlin, answers. "Wet leaves, and wood, too. Wet logs. Damp. Let's write 'damp.'" They eagerly add the word "damp" to their growing list.

At a nearby table, Nason and Christopher are examining another forest scene—in this picture the trees dominate and just a little sun filters through.

"The trees are really tall, and they're making dark shadows," exclaims Nason.

Christopher adds, "I think there are birds chirping like crazy, everywhere. It's a circus of birds!"

A low, excited hum of voices fills the room. Creative energy surges as partners build on each other's thinking. The lists of evocative words and phrases become a rich resource that students will later use to write their own poems about these scenes.

Why Is Collaborative Learning So Engaging?

Collaborative learning has long been part of many teachers' repertoire, whether students are talking and sharing ideas for a few minutes or working together over an extended period. Here are some of the reasons why.

✳ **Partners and groups provide a safe forum.** For many students, a partnership or small group feels like a safer space than the larger class group in which to try something new, make mistakes, practice being assertive, and articulate ideas. Students reluctant to speak up in a large group can find their voices in a smaller one, and the questions, comments, and new information offered by peers help them refine their ideas, clarify their thinking, and see things from new perspectives.

> **Benefits of Collaborative Learning**
>
> ➤ Provides a safe forum
>
> ➤ Helps teachers differentiate learning
>
> ➤ Meets students' need for connection

✳ **Partners and groups help you differentiate learning.** Through partnering and grouping, you can better address the range of learning styles, needs, and aptitudes found in most classrooms. When students' learning needs are met, they are more likely to feel engaged with their lessons.

* **Partners and groups meet students' need for connection.** Smaller settings provide golden opportunities for students to connect with each other. Not only are they sharing ideas and information, they're getting to know each other better and having fun together—all while accomplishing academic goals!

F A Q • **What's the most effective small group size?**

Most elementary age children can learn well in a three- or four-person group. In larger groups some children may disengage because they don't see a clear role for themselves.

As you teach throughout the day, you'll need to bring the class together in a large group for direct instruction and discussion, and you'll provide times for students to work on their own. But by weaving small group and partner work into each day's lessons, you'll promote stronger student-to-student relationships and increase overall academic engagement.

Stay Flexible When Forming Partnerships and Groups

Flexibility is key to successful collaborative work. I found that planning for partner and group work was a bit like choreographing a dance as I moved children in and out of groups of various sizes and compositions. For example:

* During reading workshop, I'd put children into **skills-based groups**; every group focused on identifying nonfiction elements, but each group was working with texts at their own "just right" levels.

* Then in writing workshop, students would choose **partners who shared their interests** and take turns critiquing each other's pieces.

* In math class, to ensure an optimal learning situation for each child, I might create a **variety of partnerships and small groups** where everyone would grapple with equivalent fractions.

* As the day wound down, a **whole-class activity** like Humdingers (see page 26) would get children moving in a way they found fun and in the process form them into small groups for a social studies learning task.

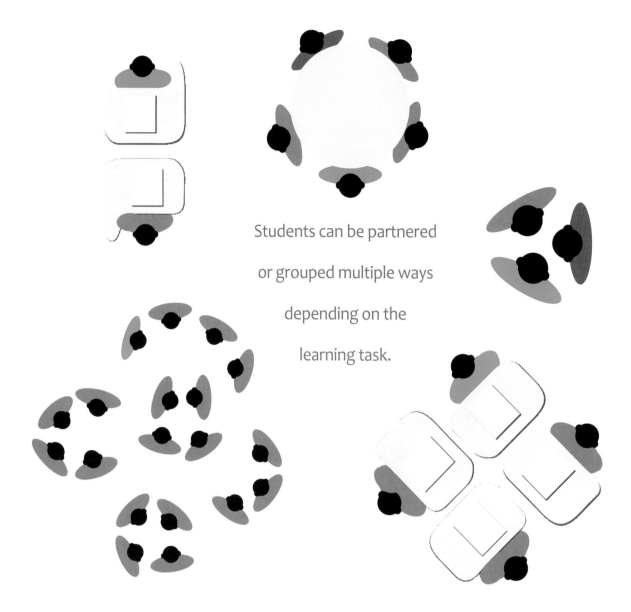

Students can be partnered
or grouped multiple ways
depending on the
learning task.

To decide on pairs and groupings, I would consider the goals of the lesson along-side students' skills and needs. What type of group would benefit each student the most? Were students ready to make thoughtful decisions when choosing their own partners? Who was working above grade level? Did some students need extra support? How many had relevant prior knowledge? Which students shared one or more interests?

The following pages offer some ideas to help you design your own classroom choreography.

Teacher-Created Groups

✴ **A first grade teacher assigns students to science exploration groups.** As he thinks about students' strengths, learning styles, and interests, he puts Jana, Sebastien, Carlos, and Marie together because he knows they're all fascinated by the butterfly chrysalis that hangs in the class terrarium. Also, Jana is a natural leader and the other three are curious, eager learners who enjoy talking and sharing with others.

✴ **A third grade teacher sets up peer response partnerships for writing workshop** by considering who will most benefit from working together. For example, she has Derek and Shawna work together because Derek has strong grammar and spelling skills, whereas Shawna's strength is imagination, and both students are good listeners who can help each other grow.

✴ In the early days of school, **a fifth grade teacher uses a Compass Partners sheet to have students match up with four different partners** (see page 25). He then calls out "Find your east partner," "Meet with your west partner," etc., when he wants students to do partner work.

✴ Before a science lesson where students will work in groups to categorize rocks, **a fourth grade teacher has them count off by sixes around the room.** She then has all ones form a group, all twos, and so on. The randomly mixed groups will enable students to experience working with lots of different classmates.

F A Q • What about similar-ability groups?

In this chapter, we talk primarily about mixed-ability groups. But you may sometimes want to create groups of students with similar learning styles or content area skills. These groups are most effective when they're short-lived and used for a specific academic or social learning goal. Once students reach the target skill or behavior, the group can change.

For example, if a few students need more practice with double-digit subtraction, they can spend some time in a small group together, perhaps with a teacher leading the group, until they've mastered the skill. Later in the week, these students can join mixed-ability pairs to play a subtraction game with double-digit numbers.

When you're forming partnerships and groups, the first thing to decide is whether you're going to assign students or use a structure that leads to more random arrangements.

Assigning partners and groups

Sometimes you need a degree of control over who works together, whether because of a lesson's content or the personality or other needs of the class. That's when you'll group and partner students intentionally, making sure that complementary skills and interests are represented in each group or partnership and that students can function together independently and stay on task.

In the opening vignette, Ms. Forsyth paired students for the brainstorming task. Although she often used random pairings or student-selected partnerships, for this activity she did the pairing because she was introducing a task—brainstorming evocative words—that she knew might be challenging for some students. By carefully selecting partners whose skills were complementary, she ensured that all students had a rewarding learning experience.

Random pairing and grouping

Teacher-created random pairings and groupings are a great way to give students experience in working with diverse classmates. Following are some fun structures and activities you can use to get students into pairs or groups. Remember to tell students in advance how they'll transition from the grouping activity to the work of the group. For instance, for Barnyard Bedlam (see facing page) you might say, "When I ring the chime, you'll stop your animal sounds, go to your tables, and begin your work."

Forming partnerships

* **Fair Sticks:** Write each student's name on one end of a craft stick. Place all the sticks into a cup with the names facing down. Pull out two sticks, and those two students become partners for the lesson or activity.

* **Matching Cards** (see activity description on page 12): Each student receives one card. Each card has a match, and students mix and mingle to find their match. Ideas for matching cards include math facts, synonyms, antonyms, states and capitals, vocabulary words and definitions, famous pairs of historical figures, numerals, letters, colors, shapes, and pictures. I found that Matching Cards was not only a great way to pair students but also a fun way to review content we were studying.

✳ **Nonverbal Lineup:** Without talking, students line up by height, birthday (month and day), or house or apartment number, smallest to largest. They can use gestures and signals, such as a show of fingers. Then they pair up with the person standing next to them in the line (or form small groups by breaking the line into segments).

✳ **Partner sheets:** Each student has a sheet on which are several items from a category: major cities, world landmarks, the seasons, compass points (see sample), etc. Students mingle, find a different partner for each item ("Will you be my West partner?"), and write each classmate's name next to the item.

Compass Partners

Your name: _____

Students keep their filled-in sheets as a reminder of who their partners are. Then you can simply say, for example, "For this activity, meet with your East partner." To form a group of four, first match up partners, then have two pairs join together. Changing partner sheets each month, or for each new unit of study, gives students opportunities to work with many classmates.

Creating small groups

✳ **Barnyard Bedlam:** Write the names of four barnyard animals on slips of paper, one animal per slip, and give one slip to each child. Students mix and mingle while making the sound of their animal and listening for others making the same sound.

When students find a match, they stand together and make the same animal sound together, until everyone is making one of four different sounds in four groups.

Optional: Have each group take turns making their animal noise while the rest of the class guesses the name of the animal.

✳ **Colored chips:** Hand out a small colored chip to each student. Students with the same colors gather together in a designated spot in the room.

✳ **Count off:** Students count off around the room by whatever number the desired group size is (fours, sixes, etc.), and then students with the same number gather together to form a group.

✳ **Humdingers:** Write the titles of four well-known songs (Happy Birthday, Old MacDonald, etc.) on slips of paper, one per slip, and give one slip to each student. Students mingle while humming the song on their slip and listening for others humming the same song. When students find a match, they stand together and hum the song in unison, until four groups are each humming a different song.

Optional: Each group takes turns humming their song while their classmates guess the name of the tune.

✳ **Picture cut-ups:** Cut each of several different images (postcards, maps, pictures of famous people or works of art, sheet music, etc.) into four pieces. Each student gets a piece of an image and searches for classmates who have the other pieces. They then put the pieces together to form the complete image. Have students do this with or without speaking—your choice.

✳ **Playing cards:** Give each student a playing card. Create groups of various sizes by having students with the same color, suit, or number gather together.

✳ **Apps and websites:** You can use a wide variety of apps and websites to form random groups as well as groups based on ability or other criteria. For example, with the app Make My Groups you can use your smartphone or tablet to create groups. Enter data about the class, the number of groups you want, and any criteria such as specific interests or ability. Then shake or tap the device, and voilà—you have teams.

Apps and websites change and are updated frequently so it's worth doing a quick Internet search to see what is currently available.

F A Q • Will older children think activities like Barnyard Bedlam and Humdingers are silly?

You, of course, know your students best and can gauge how willing they are to be playful at any given moment. In my experience, older children gladly take part in playful activities like these and enjoy the break from more serious endeavors. This is especially true when the activities are introduced enthusiastically and if students feel they're part of a safe and supportive classroom community, where it's OK to take the risk of being playful.

You can also use content that appeals to older students. In Humdingers, you could have students hum popular songs; in Barnyard Bedlam, you might list endangered species students have studied rather than farm animals.

Student-Selected Partnerships and Groups

Choosing whom to work with gives students a measure of autonomy—a key to engaged learning. Children will naturally tend to choose their best friends, who may not be their best work partners, so they'll need your help to ensure that partnerships and groups are inclusive and productive as well as engaging. Here are some ways you can do that.

Be sure you have a good foundation in place

Before you have students select their own partners or groupmates, be sure you've established an inclusive community.

When I taught fourth grade, I introduced partner selection in late fall after we'd created classroom rules that included treating each other kindly and had ample opportunities to think about what living by the rules looked like day to day. We also held daily morning meetings that helped establish a positive classroom community and provided lots of opportunities for interacting with a range of classmates.

I also gave students opportunities to practice making choices and reflecting on their experience with those choices. Early in the year, I often offered students simple choices about whom to sit next to, for example in morning meeting or during teacher read-aloud. We would discuss how to choose a partner who would help them learn and stay focused on work. We reflected on these self-selected partnerships, and students quickly learned who might be a good partner for them, even if they were not very close friends.

Start slowly and build on success

* **Start by letting children choose whom to greet or talk to.** Early in the year, build in quick, fun opportunities for this. For example, if you do a daily greeting, include some greetings where children choose whom to greet and encourage children to choose someone they don't know very well.

Then use reinforcing language (Appendix A) to support their efforts: "I saw many fourth graders greeting classmates they might not know very well. That is helping us create a welcoming and friendly classroom community."

✳ **Next, guide them in choosing work partners.** When you think children are ready for this step, begin by providing a structure for the choosing, such as Mix and Mingle to Music (p. 58). With lively music playing, students mingle; when the music stops, they partner up with someone nearby for a brief discussion or task. As with the greeting, encourage them to partner with someone they don't know well and then use reinforcing language to acknowledge their efforts.

✳ **Finally, have them choose partners in less structured ways and for longer tasks.** Do this once children are successful with brief and structured partner-choosing opportunities. You can then form small groups by having two pairs join together.

Teacher Language

How you talk with children—your words and tone—affects every aspect of your teaching and children's learning. In this book, you will see suggestions for using three kinds of teacher language:

➤ Reinforcing language, which gives specific positive feedback to children

➤ Open-ended questions, which stretch children's thinking

➤ Envisioning language, which helps children form a vision of themselves as learners

For more detailed information about these three kinds of teacher language, see Appendix A.

Teach, model, and practice

A key to successful partner and group choosing is learning how to issue and accept invitations gracefully. The strategy of Interactive Modeling (Appendix B) is a great way to teach students how to ask someone to be their partner and how to accept the invitation.

Following is an example from a third grade classroom:

"There will be times when you will have a chance to invite a classmate to be your partner," Ms. Crowe says. "Watch me as I ask Samreen to be my partner."

She looks at Samreen, who is sitting next to her, smiles, and says, "Samreen, would you be my partner today?"

Samreen responds, "Yes."

Ms. Crowe then asks the class, "What did you notice about how I invited Samreen to be my partner?"

Several students respond: "You smiled at her." "You looked right at her." "You used a friendly voice."

Ms. Crowe goes on to clarify an important point: "In this class, when someone asks you to be a partner, you say 'yes.' This is part of living by our classroom rule to treat each other in a kind and friendly way."

To underscore this point, she models how to accept an invitation to be a classmate's partner. She has a student invite her to be a partner, and she responds by saying, "Yes, thank you. I'll be your partner."

Again, Ms. Crowe asks the students what they noticed about her response.

Ms. Crowe now asks for two volunteers to model asking and accepting a lunch invitation. She calls on Danielle and Abby. The two girls sit facing each other. Danielle says, "Abby, would you be my lunch partner?" Abby responds, "Yes. Thanks!"

Ms. Crowe asks students what they noticed. They note that Danielle and Abby made eye contact and smiled at each other.

Interactive Modeling

Throughout this book, you'll see references to Interactive Modeling as a strategy you can use to quickly and effectively teach routines and skills. A seven-step process that usually takes ten to fifteen minutes, Interactive Modeling differs from traditional modeling (in which teachers demonstrate and students watch) by involving students as active participants. The teacher briefly describes what will be modeled and says why it's important, demonstrates the routine or skill, and asks for students' observations. Student volunteers then demonstrate while the rest of the class observes and notices what the volunteers are doing. Finally, all students get a chance to practice the skill or routine while the teacher coaches and gives feedback.

For a more detailed description of Interactive Modeling, see Appendix B. For an Interactive Modeling Planning Guide template, see Appendix C.

Ms. Crowe gives the class a chance to practice by having them choose lunch partners. Using a class list to keep track of whom each student asks, she calls on students one by one to invite another student to be a lunch partner.

When a student makes a misstep, she reminds them of what they just saw modeled and asks them to try again. For example, when it's Julia's turn, Julia simply says "Claire!"

Ms. Crowe stops her. "What do you need to say to her?"

"Oh, yeah," Julia says. "Can you please sit with me at lunch?"

"Yes, thanks. I'll sit with you at lunch," Claire responds.

Earlier, students had brainstormed a list of topics they could chat about at lunch, and Ms. Crowe reminds them to review the list before sending them off.

Intervene as needed

Observe students closely as they learn how to choose partners. If the same students are working together frequently, students are making choices that lead to distracted or unproductive work, or certain students are always chosen last, step in. You might need to make group assignments yourself for a while—and revisit rules for treating each other with respect.

And keep in mind that throughout the year, having children choose partners or groupmates is just one of the ways you'll form groups. Even when students are successful at keeping things kind, inclusive, and productive, you will at times want to take charge of forming the groups yourself.

Helping Students Work Together Productively

Students typically enjoy any opportunity to talk and work with classmates, and forming groups or partnerships in fun ways helps them get into a good frame of mind for learning. But for that learning to actually happen in a way that's engaging for everyone, students must know how to interact productively—to speak, listen, think, and do collaboratively. Following are ideas for providing the support and teaching the skills students need.

Managing collaborative work

You play an essential role in keeping collaborative work amicable as well as productive. As the choreographer, you not only make decisions about how to form partners and groups, you also keep the dance moving smoothly by listening, coaching, reinforcing, reminding, directing, and redirecting students' efforts to work collaboratively and helping them manage their time so that they can engage with and enjoy their learning. Here are some strategies that can help:

✴ **Coach as needed.** As students work, circulate to observe and coach, stepping in to look more closely at students' work, ask open-ended questions, offer reinforcement, and remind or redirect if students begin to go off track. To learn more about coaching students during work time, see Chapter 5.

✴ **Observe and respond.** Varying grouping and partnering structures to meet the needs of the lessons and the learners will go a long way toward supporting success with collaborative work. As you circulate and coach, observe students and use what you learn to plan for future collaborative work. What needs to change? What can stay the same? Which skills need revisiting?

How successfully students work in various kinds of groups—either teacher-created or self-selected—will depend on many factors. Events in the life of the classroom or the larger community, stressors such as testing or holidays, and the typical changes that happen as children move through developmental stages will all have an impact on their collaborative work skills.

✴ **Teach students how to ask for help.** You might find it useful to teach students how to ask for your help. For example, you might teach them to stay in their spot and raise a hand, letting them know you will respond as quickly as you can. If you think you might get pulled in a lot of directions responding to many raised hands, you might ask them to write their question or concern on a sticky note and place it in a designated spot. Let them know that you'll periodically collect the notes and respond in a timely way.

✴ **Use visual cues.** Simple visual cues can help you monitor how well students understand directions and how their work is progressing. For example, to check for understanding about directions, ask students to show thumbs-up, thumbs-down, or thumbs-in-the-middle. To see how many minutes they still need for a task, ask them to show a fist to mean zero minutes, one finger for one minute, two fingers for two minutes, and so on.

✳ **Pay attention to how you organize the classroom.** It's important to set up the classroom space so that it supports both partner and small-group work and frees children to actively connect with each other and with their work.

> ➤ **Provide a variety of work spaces** such as tables, desk clusters, open rug space, and standing work spaces.

> ➤ **Allow plenty of room,** if possible, between clusters or work spaces so children can move around the room with ease. Also, arrange desk clusters or tables so that students can easily move into and out of the spaces.

> ➤ **Make sure materials are readily available** for students' independent access.

> ➤ **Model and practice routines** that might be needed for group work, such as moving desks around or gathering materials, and any cleanup procedures that may be necessary.

Teach and practice the language of learning

Another crucial component in increasing collaboration and learning in partner and group work is teaching students a core set of thinking and communication skills—a language of learning—that helps them engage with each other and the task at hand. I learned this lesson early in my teaching career when I paired students for a math lesson without having taught them these skills. At the start, students were excited by the prospect of solving math problems with a partner and quickly worked through the first problem or two, but the partnerships soon dissolved into disagreements, hurt feelings, and little work being accomplished.

Taking the time to teach and practice the language of learning skills helps prevent or minimize problems that can arise during collaborative work, enabling students to more deeply invest themselves in their interactions and their learning.

The table below shows five categories of language of learning skills that will help students work purposefully and positively in partnerships and groups, along with specific skills they need to learn in each category.

Although this list may look daunting, keep in mind that you can efficiently teach each of these skills in the course of just about any academic lesson. And you needn't teach them all at once; you can start with just one or two and then gradually add more throughout the year. (See page 36 for a timeline suggesting when you might teach each skill.)

Listening Essentials	Speaking Essentials	Asking & Answering Questions	Crafting an Argument	Agreeing & Disagreeing
• Focusing attention • Showing interest • Sustaining attention • Developing comprehension (paraphrasing, summarizing, checking in)	• Taking turns (with partners, small groups, whole group) • Speaking confidently • Staying on topic • Speaking with clarity	• Question or statement? • Asking questions respectfully • Asking purposeful questions • Giving high-quality answers	• Speaking in an organized way • Distinguishing facts from opinions • Presenting evidence • Persuading others	• Agreeing thoughtfully • Disagreeing respectfully • Partially agreeing • Responding to disagreements

Start with essential listening skills

Before children can truly collaborate, they need to be able to hear and understand what another person says. And although older students may already seem to be capable listeners, it's still worth spending some time on these skills to ensure students can meet your specific expectations. A good way to teach listening skills is to begin by having students practice listening to a partner. Here's a way to teach that skill by using Interactive Modeling. (To learn more about Interactive Modeling, see Appendix B.)

Interactive Modeling: Listening to a Partner	
STEPS	**WHAT IT MIGHT SOUND/LOOK LIKE**
1. Say what you will model and why.	"If we want to learn a lot when we work together, we need to know how to listen closely and respectfully to each other. I'm going to do part of a Think, Pair, Share [see page 69] with Caleb to show you what that looks like. Pretend our topic is what planet we like the best and why. Caleb will tell one important fact about his favorite planet while I listen. Watch carefully and see what you notice."
2. Model the behavior.	You and Caleb sit facing each other. As Caleb speaks, you lean forward slightly, look at him, and occasionally nod. Then you speak and Caleb listens.
3. Ask students what they noticed.	"What did you notice about how Caleb and I listened to each other?" Students respond: "You took turns." "You looked at each other." "You didn't talk when the other person was talking; you just waited." "You leaned forward a little, like you really wanted to hear him." If necessary, prompt students to recall the details you want to be sure they learn: "What else did we do to show that we were listening?" "What were our hands and bodies doing while we listened?"
4. Invite one or more students to model.	"Who can show us how to listen to a partner the same way Caleb and I did?"
5. Again, ask students what they noticed.	"What did you notice about the way Trevor and Misha listened to each other?"
6. Have all students practice.	"Now we'll all practice listening just the way our volunteers did. Find your Summer partner. When I ring the chime, you'll begin. The person whose first name starts with the letter closest to the beginning of the alphabet goes first. Remember, state just one fact about why you chose your planet so that your partner will have time to talk. When I ring the chime again, wrap up what you're saying and look at me."
7. Provide feedback.	Use reinforcing language (see Appendix A) to give feedback: "I saw people looking at their partners while keeping their hands still and their voices off. Lots of people leaned forward a bit and nodded to show they were listening. Many people remembered to state just one fact. You're really getting the hang of this partner listening!"

When students are doing well with partner listening, use Interactive Modeling to teach them how to take turns listening in small groups, and give structured opportunities to practice. For example, you might assign a topic for students to speak about and have them pass a talking stick. Students talk while holding the stick; otherwise, they listen respectfully.

Tips for teaching language of learning skills

You can use this same basic progression of modeling, practicing with a partner, and then practicing in a small group to teach the other language of learning skills. And, as with the skill of listening, you can embed this teaching in your academic lessons. Here are some tips to keep in mind as you do this teaching.

* **Meet students where they are.** For example, when learning how to ask and answer questions, some students, especially young ones, may first need to learn the difference between a question and a statement. So start there; emphasize that questions often start with question words (who, what, when, why, where, and how). Interactive learning structures such as Fishbowl (p. 52), Maître d' (p. 57), and Twenty Questions (p. 71) can help you do this teaching.

* **Give positive feedback.** These are complex skills, so be empathetic when students make mistakes and use plenty of reinforcing language to recognize and encourage their efforts and successes.

* **Post anchor charts and sentence starters.** When students are first learning a skill, create (or have them create) supports to help them use the skill independently as they work in partnerships or groups. When most have become fluent with the skill, put away the supports and just use them selectively, such as when working with a student who needs a bit more practice.

* **Reteach as needed.** Rarely will children learn any skill after just one lesson; it's repeated teaching, as well as practicing, that enables them to use a skill automatically. Often, an abbreviated Interactive Modeling lesson is all that's needed (see Appendix B, p. 175).

When to Teach Language of Learning Skills
SUGGESTED TIMELINE

	Weeks 1–4	Early in year to midyear	Midyear to end of year
Grades K–2	• Focusing attention • Showing interest • Taking turns • Speaking confidently	• Sustaining attention • Developing listening comprehension skills • Speaking confidently • Core question skills • Staying on topic • Speaking with clarity • Answering questions	• Staying on topic • Speaking with clarity • Asking purposeful questions • Answering questions • Organizing thoughts • Distinguishing facts from opinions • Presenting evidence • Agreeing • Disagreeing
Grades 3–6	All K–2 skills plus: • Core question skills • Sustaining attention • Organizing thoughts	All K–2 skills plus: • Asking purposeful questions • Organizing thoughts • Distinguishing facts from opinions • Presenting evidence • Agreeing	All K–2 skills plus: • Persuading others • Partially agreeing • Responding to disagreements

Assign small group roles

Sometimes you'll find it useful to assign roles in small groups. For example, in mixed-ability small groups, one or two students may dominate while others hang back. Assigning roles ensures that each student will have a way to contribute to the group and feel part of the learning.

These roles might include:

- ✳ **Leader**—guides the group, makes sure all voices are heard, maintains focus

- ✳ **Scribe**—takes notes, compiles ideas on a graphic organizer, charts ideas, or does other writing tasks

- ✳ **Timekeeper**—keeps track of time

- ✳ **Presenter**—shares finished work or ideas with the larger group or other audience

- ✳ **Materials manager**—gathers and returns needed supplies

You might assign these jobs to specific children, with an eye to balancing strengths while helping children stretch and grow. At other times, you might randomly assign roles. This will help rotate responsibilities among students so they can develop and practice a wide variety of skills needed for successful group work. Write each role on a slip of paper and then have children draw the slips out of a box, or use a strategy such as Fair Sticks (see page 24) to draw children's names and then match the names to the roles.

Finally, roles can be self-selected by students when you think they're ready to choose a role they can carry out effectively.

Define expectations

However you choose to assign roles, clearly define the expectations and responsibilities for each one. And before students take on these roles, model what each role is and how to do it. Some teachers find it helpful to post an anchor chart of how each role looks and sounds when performed well.

Reinforce students' taking responsibility for their work

You'll also want to emphasize that students should take responsibility for their own work within the group. This means carrying out their responsibilities and allowing other group members to carry out theirs. Remember to reinforce students' positive efforts and let them know why their efforts matter to the group. For example: "Everyone completed their individual tasks. That made it possible for you to work successfully as a team on the final part of the assignment."

Use role-playing to address problem areas

Group work can present students with situations in which they need to make a decision about a course of action. For example, how do they share limited materials equitably? How do they come to consensus when they have a range of opinions?

If you become aware of situations that interrupt productive group work—or you anticipate this happening—you can use the strategy of role-playing. Role-playing takes fifteen to twenty minutes and is worth the time investment, since it will help you head off problems or keep them from becoming bigger.

In role-playing, you describe the scenario, stopping just before the point of possible problems. You ask for ideas about how to address the situation in ways that are respectful to everyone involved and follow the class rules, and students then role-play these proposed solutions. The emphasis throughout is on gathering students' ideas for solutions and trying out only those that will help resolve the situation.

Here's what role-playing might look like in a fifth grade classroom:

⁕ **Describe a specific situation.** Ms. Harmon brings students to the meeting area and says, "Later today in social studies you'll be working in your data-gathering groups to begin compiling your report on the neighborhood you studied. You've collected interesting data and you'll need to make several decisions about how to summarize and represent it.

"Imagine that I'm a fifth grader sitting with my group. I've worked hard to gather this data and I know that reporting it accurately is important.

"I've shared my data with the group and the scribe has written down a summary of what I said, but I don't agree with how she summarized it—I think her words have changed my meaning."

* **Name the positive goal.** Ms. Harmon continues, "Our rules say that we will treat each other with respect and that we will help each other do our best learning. How can I disagree in a way that's respectful and that moves the learning forward?"

* **Invite and record students' ideas for solutions.** Students begin to call out ideas and Ms. Harmon writes them on the board, making sure to reframe any "don't do this" ideas into positive statements. Here are a few of the students' suggestions:

"You could say, 'Hmm, I'm not sure that's exactly what I meant. Can I clarify my statement?'"

"That's an interesting idea. It's not quite what I meant but I'd like to know more about what you think."

"I wonder if this word is exactly right. How about saying _____? That might be closer to what I meant."

* **Act out one idea with yourself in the lead role.** Ms. Harmon asks for volunteers to play the roles of the other three group members. She takes the lead role for this first role-play and chooses the third option of wondering about one word in the summary.

* **Ask students what they noticed.** After she finishes, she asks the audience, "What did you notice?"

Hands quickly go up and Ms. Harmon calls on several students, who offer astute observations:

"You were calm."

"You didn't sound mad—you just were matter-of-fact."

"You were friendly, like you were all working on this together."

Ms. Harmon then turns to the student who played the scribe. "How did it feel when I disagreed with you?"

The student responds, "It felt fine. You weren't mad or anything. You just wanted to make sure I got it right." The other group members nod.

* **Act out other ideas; consider having a student play the lead role.** The role-play continues, working through the options listed on the chart. Ms. Harmon now has students take the lead role—if students were younger or less experienced with role-playing, she might have continued playing the lead part.

* **Summarize lessons learned and follow up.** At the end of the role-playing Ms. Harmon says, "Today in social studies, I'll be checking in to see how each group is doing. I know you'll find ways to express any disagreement respectfully and come to a solution."

For a Role-Play Planning Guide template, see Appendix C.

FINAL THOUGHT: COLLABORATION BENEFITS LEARNING

Research confirms what we've observed in our years of teaching: Great cognitive growth happens when students have opportunities to interact socially in safe and structured ways. Through partner and group work, you can offer students many such opportunities. You'll find that they'll learn more broadly and more deeply, while also developing the social-emotional skills essential for their success in middle school, high school, and beyond.

3

Making Learning Interactive

In a sixth grade classroom, students pair up to read an article on Mesopotamia from their social studies text using the Say Something structure (p. 65). They read a paragraph together, take turns saying one key thing they learned from that paragraph, and then continue to the next paragraph.

Daryl and Sita each read the first paragraph silently. "Settling near a river was a good decision," Daryl says.

Sita responds, "But Mesopotamia didn't have forests or mountains. Don't you need wood for fires and for building houses?"

Some pairs are reading aloud to each other; others, like Daryl and Sita, choose to read silently. All are engaged in their reading and thinking, sharing observations and wonderings about what they've read.

Down the hall in a second grade classroom, students are wrapping up a unit on community during which they've focused on their own town. Working in pairs, they've drawn maps indicating key landmarks and institutions. They hang the maps in the hall outside their classroom and then take part in a Museum Walk (p. 59), strolling and pausing to study each map.

Excited "oohs" and "aahs" emerge as children view their classmates' maps. "That's my house in that map!" Ashleigh exclaims.

"Wow. Our school is really close to the fire station," says DeShawn.

Mapmakers ask each other about techniques ("How did you get the river to look so shiny?") and comment on choices ("You really put in a lot of animals!"). After the Museum Walk, they head back to their seats with plenty of ideas for their next project—a map of their entire state.

We know that rich, deep learning happens when children can move and talk, dig into content, and try things out as they collaborate with and learn from peers. But for these engagements with content and with each other to be productive, children need structures to help them work in ways that are safe and orderly as well as fun. Interactive learning structures like those used in the opening vignettes provide that safety, order, and fun. Plus, they help students practice essential listening, speaking, and thinking skills and key social skills such as cooperation and responsibility.

In this chapter, you'll learn over two dozen interactive learning structures that you can use to get students moving, thinking, and learning together. You'll find tips on planning for, setting up, and using interactive learning structures, along with guidance on which structures work best for the opening, body, and closing of typical lessons.

Benefits of Interactive Learning Structures

➤ Provide safe ways for students to interact

➤ Give students fun but orderly ways to dig into content

➤ Provide practice in essential listening, speaking, and thinking skills

➤ Help students practice key social skills such as cooperation and responsibility

Keys to Success With Interactive Learning Structures

Some of the structures you'll learn about in this chapter are simple to set up and facilitate; others are a bit more complex. All will benefit from careful introduction and facilitation. Here are some tips to ensure success:

Teach and use a signal for quiet attention. Engaged learning is not always quiet learning! The hum of conversation and rustle of movement is often a welcome sign that children are active and interactive. But sometimes you'll want to get students' quiet attention, for example, to give a new set of directions or let them know an activity is about to end. Instead of relying on students' hearing you say "OK, quiet down now!" try using a signal for quiet that you've taught and practiced with the children ahead of time.

Signals can be either silent, such as a raised hand, or auditory, such as a chime or bell. Silent signals work well when students are gathered together and can easily see you. Auditory signals are best when students are working in different parts of the room, especially if the activity involves conversation.

Use Interactive Modeling early in the year to teach the signals. Once you've done the initial teaching, practice the signals frequently until most students are responding quickly and quietly. Be sure to reinforce students' quick response. For example: "When I rang the chime, I saw you all finish what you were saying and then quietly turn to look at me. That will help us move on to the next set of directions." Use the signals consistently whenever you need to get quiet attention. (See page 46 for an example of using Interactive Modeling to teach a signal.)

Plan how you'll teach each structure. As you prepare to teach an interactive learning structure, think about which skills students already use successfully and which might be challenging and require modeling and support. Suppose, for example, that before using the Say Something structure described in the opening vignette, you realize that students will need help staying on topic and sharing only one key thing they've learned. When you introduce the structure, make sure to model saying just one key point and have children practice this with partners. During the activity, circulate and coach partners when you hear them beginning to stray off topic or engage in longer conversations.

It's also a good idea to use familiar content when you introduce a new structure. That keeps the focus on learning how to take part in the structure, rather than trying to learn new content. Then, when you are ready to use the same structure for more challenging work, students already know the structure, so they can focus on the content.

Give clear directions. Clear, concise directions will do much to ensure success with interactive learning structures. Break the directions down into manageable steps and give just a few steps at a time. When children have completed those steps, give a few more. For example, when introducing the Circle Maps structure (p. 51), in which students work with a small group to brainstorm ideas and then switch "idea maps" with another group, you might give directions for the brainstorming, and when students have completed that step, give directions for the next step—switching maps.

Consider giving directions both verbally and in writing. I often posted written directions to give extra support and facilitate greater independence. Instead of asking me to repeat steps, children could refer to the chart and self-correct.

Interactive Modeling: Teaching a Signal for Quiet

Fourth grade teacher Mr. Furst says, "In lessons this year, we'll often be moving around and talking with each other. When I need to get your attention, I'll use a signal, like this." He rings the chime. "When I ring the chime, you need to bring what you're doing to a close and quietly turn and look at me. I'm going to demonstrate. Notice what I do."

Mr. Furst hands the chime to Paula, who has agreed to ring it. He pretends to be busy with a task. When Paula rings the chime, he stops what he is doing and quietly turns to look at Paula.

"What did you notice?" he asks the students.

"You stopped quickly."

"You turned to look at her."

"You were quiet."

"Can someone else show us how to respond to the chime just like I did?" Mr. Furst asks. Manuel volunteers and carefully follows the same steps that Mr. Furst did.

"What did you notice Manuel do?" Students note that he stopped what he was doing when he heard the chime and turned quietly toward Mr. Furst.

"Now you're all going to get a chance to practice. Turn and talk with a neighbor about something you did after school yesterday."

Students begin chatting. After a few minutes, Mr. Furst rings the chime. Within a few seconds, all students are turned to face him.

"You ended your conversations and quietly faced me. That lets us all move on to the next activity."

Provide time limits. As part of giving directions, give clear time limits—and then stick to them. "You'll be doing a Museum Walk to look at each other's maps of our community. You'll have five minutes to walk around and view the maps. I'll ring the chime when it's time to wrap up and come to the meeting circle." For activities that require cleanup of materials or rearrangement of furniture, give a "time is almost up" signal to let children know that they need to finish their work and clean up.

Have materials ready. Be sure pens, pencils, markers, chart paper, sticky notes, and other materials are available and easily accessible to students. Also, check that students know the routines for getting supplies they might need and for returning them at the close of the activity.

Interactive Learning Structures to Try

In the following pages, you'll find directions for a number of interactive learning structures. Here are some things to think about when deciding which interactive learning structure to use.

* **The purpose of the lesson.** The introduction to each structure notes how it can help students meet various learning goals. For example, if students are just beginning to learn about a topic, you might use Say Something (p. 65) or Jigsaw (p. 56), which help students take in new information. Are students building their knowledge of a topic? A structure such as Circle Maps (p. 51) or Paired Verbal Fluency (p. 61) can help them dig in more deeply.

* **Student readiness.** Any structure you choose should be relatively easy for all students to use successfully so the structure supports rather than interferes with learning goals. For example, an interactive learning structure might require students to write on chart paper, move safely around the room, or wait their turn to speak while listening to a partner. Can all students do those things?

* **Movement and social interaction.** Would movement be most helpful during the start of the lesson, in the middle, or at the end? Where might social interaction best support learning?

* **Timing.** Some interactive learning structures are quick; others require more time to set up and do. Do you have time before the lesson to create sort cards? Can you set aside enough time during the lesson for groups to visit all the charts in a Carousel (p. 50)?

* **Space.** Do you have room for groups of students to create Circle Maps (p. 51) on large pieces of chart paper? Can students move safely to four separate places in the classroom for a Four Corners (p. 53) activity? Will everyone have space to mingle during Info Exchange (p. 54)?

Interactive Learning Structure Planning Chart

To help you choose structures quickly, the following chart gives broad grade ranges indicating when children typically have the skills required to use the structure. Keep in mind, though, that most of these structures can be adapted for any age or grade. Additionally, to help you get started, the structures are categorized according to when in a lesson you might use them. As you become familiar with the structures, use them wherever they'll help students meet learning goals.

Structures to Use in Opening a Lesson

Structures to Use in the Body of a Lesson

*World Café™ is a registered trademark of World Café Community Foundation, Greenbrae, CA, 94904, www.theworldcafe.com.

Structures to Use in Closing a Lesson

CARD SORT

To reach a shared understanding of a topic, small groups of students sort into categories cards that are printed with topic-related scenarios or facts.

Skills practiced: Cooperation, sorting and categorizing, working toward consensus, sharing an opinion or point of view, listening

Directions

1. Form groups of three or four students, distribute the sort cards, and tell students the categories.

2. In each group, students read a scenario or fact from the top card, discuss which category it fits, and place the card in a designated spot on the table. They then read the next card and sort it.

3. Allow ten minutes for groups to read and sort.

4. Have each group read one card aloud, say which category they chose for that card, and briefly explain why.

Tips for Success

• Think of categories related to a topic. For example, if the topic is plants, the categories could include types of plants, parts of a plant, and what kinds of soil different plants need.

• Think of scenarios, facts, or words related to the topic and print them on index cards. In the preceding example, the cards could include words such as flowers, weeds, trees, loam, roots, leaves, and stems.

• You'll need enough cards for each small group to have four or five cards.

• Before the activity, model with a partner how to decide which category a card might go into. Discuss what you might do if a card seems to fit in more than one category.

CAROUSEL

Try this activity when you need to explore a topic in depth in a short amount of time. In small groups, students circulate around the room brainstorming ideas and writing them on posted chart paper. When they complete the carousel, each chart contains ideas from all of the groups.

Skills practiced: Cooperation, brainstorming for ideas, listening, making connections

Directions

1. Form groups of three or four students. Designate a scribe for each group and give a different-colored marker to each scribe.

2. Each group visits a chart and brainstorms ideas about the topic; the scribe records the ideas on the chart.

3. At a signal, each group rotates to the next chart and adds to the ideas listed.

4. Continue until all groups have visited each chart.

Tips for Success

• Post charts around the room. Label each chart with a subtopic of the topic being considered. For example, if the topic is Native Americans, the subtopics might be homes, food, clothing, symbolism, famous Native Americans, tribes, and tools.

• Make sure all students understand the focus for brainstorming. Give examples if necessary.

• Model safe movement.

• Make sure scribes bring their markers with them as the groups move from chart to chart.

• Let students know how much time they'll have at each chart. If you think students are running out of ideas or getting restless, shorten time at the charts.

CIRCLE MAPS

These maps help students look at different perspectives on a topic and synthesize information.

Skills practiced: Categorizing, brainstorming, cooperation, synthesizing information

Directions

1. Form groups of three or four students. Give each group a piece of chart paper and designate a scribe for each group.

2. The scribe draws a big circle on the paper and writes the assigned topic—for example, insects—in the middle of the circle.

3. As the group brainstorms ideas and facts about the topic, the scribe writes these within the circle.

4. At the end of a designated time (for example, ten minutes), each group swaps maps with a neighboring group.

5. The recipients categorize the information and provide a key to their categories. For example, for the topic "insects" categories might be types, food, life cycle, homes, and body parts.

6. Groups then swap the maps again and read and reflect on the categories.

Tips for Success

• Make sure all students know the focus for brainstorming and understand how to do the categorization task. Give examples if necessary.

• Model safe movement of the maps between groups at swap time.

• Give each group a different-colored marker.

FISHBOWL

To reinforce skills the class is learning or knowledge they're gaining, a few students hold a brief mock discussion or demonstration while the rest of the class observes. Afterward, students note key words they heard or actions they observed.

Skills practiced: Speaking and listening skills, using multiple skills at the same time (such as paraphrasing and expressing partial agreement), using skills learned in one context (such as how to describe a sequential process in language arts) in another (such as math or science)

Directions

1. Prepare the students who will be in the Fishbowl to make sure they can demonstrate the skills or share the knowledge you want to reinforce.

2. Tell the class what to observe. For example: "Watch how your classmates demonstrate backing up their ideas with reasons and evidence."

3. Students demonstrate and classmates watch while you coach as needed.

4. After the demonstration, guide the class discussion to make sure all key points are covered.

5. Give the whole class a chance to discuss what they've heard or to practice the skills they've seen demonstrated, or invite volunteers to do another Fishbowl.

Tips for Success

• Choose a topic that students are interested in or familiar with so they can more easily focus on what they're seeing and hearing.

• Keep it brief—no more than five minutes.

• Choose students purposefully, but be inclusive over time.

• Take part if needed to ensure key skills are included and the conversation or demonstration flows smoothly.

Grouping students according to their preferences or opinions can spark discussions, help students reflect about a variety of topics, and give them a chance to share ideas on topics they care about.

Skills practiced: Making connections, making a choice, sharing ideas with others

Directions

1. Pose a question to the group and provide four possible responses. Designate one corner of the room for each response.

2. Students move to the corner of their choice.

3. In the corners, students discuss the response their corner represents. They can do this as a small group or in pairs.

Tips for Success

- Decide on the question and possible responses.

  – You might ask a question about aspects of a topic they're studying. ("Which type of fiction do you like best—historical, mystery, fantasy, or humor—and why?")

  – You might present a current event and possible opinions. ("Which environmental issue should be a priority for our city to research and invest in—recycling, alternative forms of transportation such as bicycles or electric cars, alternative forms of energy such as solar or wind, or water conservation?")

- Give students some think time before releasing them to choose a corner.

- Model safe movement.

- Before students go to their chosen corner, let them know whether they'll discuss their response with a small group or a partner.

- Give a focus question for discussion within each corner group; for example, "What's the one big reason you love the genre you chose?" or "What's one book you think might convince other classmates to like your favorite type of fiction?"

Classroom Snapshot

Four Corners • The fifth graders are bursting with ideas, questions, and opinions after listening to the latest chapter of *Treasure Island*. "OK," says their teacher, Mr. Marquette. "Let's share ideas about Jim Hawkins."

He points to words taped in the corners of the room and says: "You'll go to that corner if you think the best description of Jim is 'rebellious,' that one for 'adventurous,' this one for 'foolish,' and the last corner for 'brave.' Once you get to your corner, take turns answering this question: Why does the word you chose best describe Jim? Remember to use examples from the book to support your opinions."

When Mr. Marquette rings the chime, students scatter to their chosen corners and eagerly begin their conversations.

INFO EXCHANGE

This activity is a fun way to share ideas and deepen learning about a topic.

Skills practiced: Staying focused, working with a range of classmates, succinctly sharing information, listening carefully

Directions

1. Distribute index cards with facts or quotes written on them—one card to each student.

2. Invite students to mingle and find a partner. Partners read their quotes or facts to each other and discuss them briefly.

3. After both partners have shared, they swap cards, find new partners, and repeat the process for several more rounds.

Tips for Success

- Write facts or quotes related to a topic on index cards or slips of paper—one for each student (it's OK to duplicate quotes or facts).

- Give a focus for the discussion, such as "What is a connection you make to this information?" or "What question does this information raise for you?"

- Model safe movement.

This conversation structure is a good way to share information that doesn't require in-depth discussion or to do a quick reflection on an activity or topic.

Skills practiced: Listening, turn-taking, staying focused and brief when speaking

Directions

1. Students count off by twos. Ones form a circle, facing out; twos form a circle facing the ones so everyone has a partner.

3. Give a topic for discussion. Partners take turns speaking—allow about one minute for each partner.

4. Give a new topic. Direct students in one of the circles to take a step to their right or left so that everyone has a new partner with whom to discuss the new topic.

Tips for Success

- Model how to move safely into the circles.

- Use an established signal for quiet to get attention before directing students in one of the circles to move.

- Give students the next topic to discuss before directing them to move so they can immediately begin talking with their new partners.

Classroom Snapshot

Inside-Outside Circles • The last few second graders hang up their smocks and join their classmates in the circle. Mrs. Linworth smiles as she looks around at the group. "I saw artists working hard at their easels today. Some of you painted pictures; others experimented with lines and shapes. Let's do Inside-Outside Circles so you can share ideas with your classmates."

The children count off, and then form the two circles. "Now take turns telling each other one thing you learned today about working with acrylic paints."

"I learned you can smear them with your fingers," Jocelyn says. Her partner, Manuel, nods. "I mixed too many colors together," he says. "It looked icky."

Around the circle, other pairs are exchanging ideas in a similar way. Mrs. Linworth rings the chime, names a new topic, the outer circle takes one step to the right, and the children begin exchanging ideas with their new partner.

JIGSAW

Students work in small groups to become knowledgeable about one aspect of a topic or one part of a long text. Then they share their knowledge in "jigsaw" groups that fit together the bits of knowledge like pieces in a puzzle.

Skills practiced: Listening, finding main ideas, summarizing, sharing ideas with others

Directions

1. Divide the class into knowledge groups of three or four students and assign each group a piece of text to read.

2. After reading, knowledge groups discuss key ideas.

3. Regroup the class into jigsaw groups with at least one representative from each knowledge group.

4. New groups share key ideas with each other.

Tips for Success

• Consider creating a note-taking sheet for both the knowledge and jigsaw groups.

• To reduce confusion when grouping, use different names for the two sets of groups (for example, A, B, C for the knowledge groups and 1, 2, 3 for the jigsaws).

• Be clear about the purpose for reading so that the knowledge groups pay attention to key ideas.

MAÎTRE D'

The teacher invites students to "tables" of various sizes, where they exchange ideas on a topic. This is a good activity for helping students share a range of ideas or opinions.

Skills practiced: Listening, turn-taking, staying focused and brief when speaking, moving carefully

Directions

1. Activity begins with students standing in a circle. You call out a grouping (for example, "Table for two") and students form groups with the specified number of members.

2. Give a topic for discussion. Let students know how long they'll have to share.

3. When time is up, announce a new table grouping and new topic.

Tips for Success

- Create your list of discussion topics for the different groupings.

- Use a signal to get attention when it's time to move to a new group.

- Consider giving a thirty-second warning before inviting students to move to a new group.

- Model how to move safely and efficiently into new groupings.

In this lively activity, students have a chance to gather ideas and information from several partners. This is a useful way to share learning about a topic—and to get children moving.

Skills practiced: Listening, turn-taking, staying focused and brief when speaking, moving carefully

Directions

1. Before doing the activity, students gather information, examples, techniques, or strategies related to a topic.

2. With notes in hand, students move around the room while music plays.

3. When the music stops, they find a partner and each shares one idea or piece of information.

4. Repeat for several rounds.

Tips for Success

• Give students time to consolidate key learning, facts, and ideas before doing the activity.

• Consider providing a note-taking sheet.

• Choose music that's lively enough to energize but not so lively that self-control is challenged.

• Model safe and efficient movement.

MUSEUM WALK

Students get a chance to display and view recently completed work or brainstormed lists as they share information, reflect on a project, or summarize learning.

Skills practiced: Reading for important information and main ideas, sharing ideas with others, answering focus questions

Directions

1. Direct students to walk around and look at the items displayed.

2. Give a focus for viewing; for example, if students are viewing timelines of the lives of famous Americans, you might ask them to discover how old each person was when they made an important contribution, or have them consider each person's educational experiences.

3. You can encourage students to take notes on what they see.

4. After a few minutes, gather the group together and ask a few people to share their observations.

Tips for Success

• Post—or have students post—items you want students to see.

• Consider providing a note-taking sheet.

• Model safe movement.

This small-group discussion activity encourages careful listening. It's a good way for students to dig more deeply into a topic and share what they learn.

Skills practiced: Listening, summarizing or paraphrasing, staying focused on a topic

Directions

1. Divide students into groups of three or four and have them count off within each group.

2. Give a topic for discussion. Let students know that any one of them might need to report to the large group, so they all need to listen carefully.

3. Give several minutes for the discussion and then signal for attention.

4. Call out a number (for example, two).

5. The person with that number in each group summarizes what their group discussed.

6. Repeat, calling out different numbers.

Tips for Success

- To help everyone pay attention to and remember key ideas, be clear about the purpose for the discussion and sharing.

- Review skills needed for careful listening and appropriate sharing (brief, on topic, voice loud enough for all to hear, etc.).

- Teach students what to do if they need help or more support from their group when they are the one called on to share a summary.

Classroom Snapshot

Numbered Heads Together • Sixth grade teacher Mr. Trobaugh has divided the class into groups of four and asked students to count off in each group and remember their number. He's given directions for them to discuss the results of their research about the human impact on climate change.

Discussions are lively as students share ideas and information. As they talk, Mr. Trobaugh circulates, listening in, guiding, and supporting as needed with reminders about group discussion rules.

After five minutes or so, he rings the chime. "I heard respectful and reasoned disagreement as well as agreement on this challenging topic." The students smile and nod at each other. "Now," he continues, "all the number threes will summarize their group's discussion for us. Who'd like to go first?"

This sharing structure helps partners consider a topic in more depth and ensures both partners have an equal chance to talk.

Skills practiced: Focusing on one idea, speaking succinctly, listening carefully, responding to others' ideas

Directions

1. Students pair up (you can use random pairings or assign partners).

2. Each pair decides who will be A and who will be B.

3. Give a focus for discussion, such as why a character in a book acted in a certain way.

4. In round one, person A talks for one minute and person B listens; then person B talks for one minute and person A listens.

5. Signal for attention and then begin round two. Now person A talks for forty seconds and person B listens; then they switch.

6. Signal for attention; then begin round three, in which partners speak for twenty seconds.

7. Partners reflect together on what they heard each other say.

Tips for Success

- If you're going to assign partners intentionally, figure out the pairings in advance.

- If you're going to assign partners randomly, plan how you'll do that.

- Model how to focus on one idea when responding to the focus question.

- Model how to listen respectfully.

POPCORN

In this fun way of reviewing prior knowledge or reflecting on learning, students "pop up" to speak to the larger group.

Skills practiced: Speaking to the whole group, waiting for a natural pause in a conversation to speak up.

Directions

1. Students sit in a circle.

2. Give a topic and focus for sharing.

3. When a student is ready to respond, she "pops up" and shares her idea.

4. After she shares, she remains standing and another student pops up and shares.

5. If one student shares an idea that another student was thinking of, the second student pops up in silent agreement.

6. If two students pop up at the same time, they both sit down and try again until just one pops up at a time.

Tips for Success

• Choose a topic that students have prior experience with or have been studying. Frame it in a way that leads to brief, concise responses. For example, if you've been studying Martin Luther King, Jr., ask students to share one word or phrase from his "I Have a Dream" speech that they think is powerful or that they connect with.

• Model safe movement when "popping up."

• Discuss what to do when two or more people pop up at once.

• Before starting the activity, give students think time and recommend that they think of a couple of possible responses.

PROS AND CONS

Partners debate the pros and cons as they look more deeply into a topic and view it from several perspectives.

Skills practiced: Arguing for a position, using logic and evidence to support an argument, listening carefully and respectfully to differing views

Directions

1. Place students in pairs. Have them decide who is A and who is B.

2. Let students know that A's will take the pro position and B's will take the con position.

3. Read aloud a provocative opinion.

4. After a brief period for everyone to think, each pair debates the stated position:

   • The pro person takes one minute to list all the reasons for her side.

   • The con person does the same.

   • Both students have thirty seconds to respond to each other, supporting their ideas with evidence and logic.

5. Debrief with the whole class, focusing on which reasons each side found most compelling.

Tips for Success

• Choose a provocative opinion based on a topic the class is studying or an issue that's relevant for students. For example:

   — Sixth graders should have a recess break every afternoon.

   — All students should wear uniforms to school.

   — In the novel *Sounder*, sending the father to jail for stealing the ham was the right thing to do.

   — The United States should increase funding for space exploration programs.

• Acknowledge the challenge of articulating a position you might not agree with. Let students know that it's a good way to really understand different points of view.

• If necessary, model giving both a pro and a con statement.

• Consider using an anchor chart with sample language students can use when stating pros and cons.

Students gather information by circulating and looking at displays of information or brainstormed lists.

Skills practiced: Reading for important information or main ideas, recording and organizing ideas.

Directions

1. Direct students to silently walk around and read the displayed facts or information and take notes on what they see.

2. After a few minutes, gather the group together and ask a few people to share their observations.

Tips for Success

- Post, or have students post, information you want them to see: for example, facts about a topic in science or key events in a period of history.

- Provide a note-taking sheet or graphic organizer.

- Model safe movement.

- Model the use of the note-taking sheet or graphic organizer.

This is a useful structure for gaining a deeper understanding of a topic.

Skills practiced: Speaking concisely, staying on topic

Directions

1. Place students in pairs. Have them read a small portion of text (or listen to a short video or audio clip).

2. Partners decide together how far to read, view, or listen before pausing to "say something."

3. At the pause, each partner says one thing (a comment or question) related to what they read, saw, or heard. Their statements or questions do not need to relate to each other.

4. Repeat this process until students have worked through the text or clip. Students can then have a conversation about the whole text or clip and respond to any questions or comments.

Tips for Success

- Choose a portion of text or a clip that easily divides into sections.

- Model how to make one focused statement or question.

- Model respectful listening.

SCAVENGER HUNT

Students do a "scavenger hunt" for key ideas in a book, article, website, or other resource as a way to learn new information and engage with content. This activity helps students focus on particular points or important elements of the content.

Skills practiced: Using nonfiction text features to locate information, paying attention to detail, scanning text, reading for information

Directions

1. Give students a list of items to look for—the list could be posted on a whiteboard or printed on paper and distributed.

2. Allow students time to look for the listed items. Students can check off each item as they find it.

3. Use the list to prompt a whole-class discussion. You can talk about each point on the list (where that item was found in the resource, what connections it has to the topic, etc.).

Tips for Success

• Decide on three to six items you want students to look for in the designated resource. For example, if students are studying the solar system, you might have them look for specific facts about the planets, or find where they could compare the sizes of planets.

• Have resources available and ready for use and create a checklist of items to look for.

• Model how to find information in the resource and what to do when they find an item on the list.

• Let students work with a partner.

Classroom Snapshot

Scavenger Hunt • An occasional squeal of delight punctuates the classroom hum as the first graders explore nonfiction books about whales, outer space, dancing, and their many other interests.

After a minute or so, Ms. Madison rings the chime and waits for students' quiet attention. "I see that you're enjoying getting to know your nonfiction books," she says. "Now let's do a scavenger hunt!"

She points to a large chart on which she's written Table of Contents, Index, and Photograph.

"Yesterday, we talked about these parts of nonfiction books. When I ring the chime, you'll look for each part in your book and mark it with a sticky note. Thumb up when you're ready to start."

Soon, all thumbs are up and students begin intently flipping through pages and marking their finds with sticky notes.

SNOWBALL

This is a fun way to reflect on a topic.

Skills practiced: Summarizing, articulating thoughts

Directions

1. Gather students in a circle and give them each a piece of paper.

2. Each student writes a short response to a focus question. They do not need to write their names.

3. Students crumple their papers into "snowballs."

4. On your signal, students toss their snowballs into the center of the circle.

5. Students then pick up a snowball close to them and take turns reading their snowballs aloud.

6. You can close with brief group reflection on common themes, intriguing ideas, etc.

Tips for Success

- Give an example of the kind of response you expect.

- Model safe movement in the circle.

- Remind students how to share with a voice loud enough for everyone to hear; model for them if necessary.

Students gather information, examples, techniques, strategies, or evidence and then share with several partners.

Skills practiced: Speaking with a number of partners, staying on topic

Directions

1. Prompt students with an open-ended question. For example, in a lesson on 3-D shapes, you might ask, "How are 3-D shapes different from 2-D shapes?" or "Where in our classroom do you see specific 3-D shapes [cube, sphere, etc.]?"

2. Students work alone to gather the information.

3. After a specified time, students mingle and swap ideas.

Tips for Success

• Provide a structure for gathering and recording ideas before the Swap Meet.

• Provide a note-taking sheet to use during the Swap Meet.

• Emphasize that students swap just one idea before moving on to another person.

• Model safe movement.

Classroom Snapshot

Swap Meet • "OK, scientists," Mr. Ellis says to the kindergartners gathered around him. "Time for our plant observations! As you look at the bean plants, think about why some bean plants might be taller than others. Begin your observations when I ring the chime and come back to the circle when I ring it again."

After a few minutes of close observation, Mr. Ellis rings the chime and the students return to the circle.

Mr. Ellis says, "I saw people looking closely at the plants, so I bet you have lots of ideas about why some grew so tall. When I ring the chime, stand and find one person to share one idea with."

He rings the chime again and students stand. They quickly find a partner and share observations. Melinda pairs up with Zahir. "I think the ones that are in a sunny spot are growing taller," she says. Zahir nods and says, "Yeah. I think so, too. And maybe someone watered them more!"

THINK, PAIR, SHARE

To dig deeper into a topic or reflect on all they've learned, students engage in focused conversation with a partner and then share key ideas with the whole group.

Skills practiced: Listening, staying on topic, summarizing key ideas

Directions

1. Pair students up. Name a topic or ask an open-ended question.

2. Give students a minute or two to think about their response.

3. Partners then talk for a few minutes, each sharing their response to the question or topic.

4. When they're ready to share with the whole group, they raise their hands.

5. When most hands are up, give a thirty-second warning to finish up.

6. Invite one person from each pair to share a key idea from their discussion.

Tips for Success

- Prepare topics/open-ended questions.

- Let students know that they will be sharing key ideas with the whole group and direct them to identify the spokesperson in each pair.

- Consider providing a structure, such as ringing a chime halfway through the discussion time, to ensure that both partners have time to talk.

- Model how to talk and listen in focused partner discussions.

Students choose an opinion on a topic and discuss their thinking with a partner.

Skills practiced: Stating and supporting an opinion

Directions

1. Students gather in a circle that you've divided in half with a piece of string or tape.

2. Read two opinion statements about a topic the class is studying. For example, "Christopher Columbus was a brave hero" and "Christopher Columbus was an ordinary person who made mistakes."

3. Designate which half of the circle represents each opinion.

4. At a signal, students move. If they:

   • Agree with both statements, they stand on the center line.

   • Agree with only one statement, they move to the appropriate half of the circle.

   • Disagree with both statements, they stand outside the circle.

5. Students find a partner—either someone who made the same choice as they did or a different choice.

6. Brainstorm as many facts as they can to support their opinion(s).

7. Ask a few students to share their thinking with the whole group. Any student whose thinking is changed by the discussion can change places in the circle.

Tips for Success

• Model safe movement.

• Model how to have a focused partner discussion.

TWENTY QUESTIONS

Use this structure not just to review content but also as a fun way to practice asking and answering questions. This is usually a whole-group activity, but you can pair students up or form small groups and then have the partnership or group ask questions or guess at answers.

Skills practiced: Recalling information, asking questions to learn more, listening carefully

Directions

1. Designate a leader. The leader thinks of a person, place, event, or topic that the class has been studying and gives a clue. For example: "I'm thinking of a character from a book we read last month."

2. The class can ask up to twenty questions to try to figure out the answer.

3. Students may guess at any time. After two incorrect guesses, the leader reveals the correct answer.

4. Name a new leader and repeat as time permits.

Tips for Success

• The first few times you do this activity, take the leader role yourself.

• If you're having a student lead the activity, work with them ahead of time to frame the clue.

• Consider setting parameters on the questions such as:

— Allow only yes or no questions—or avoid yes or no questions

— Questions that start with a specific question word, such as what, where, when, who

— Questions that can be answered in just one sentence

• Model asking effective questions.

Students use Venn diagrams to compare and contrast information on a topic and to show relationships between items, ideas, or people. They can also use them to record personal differences and similarities as a way to get to know each other better.

Skills practiced: Comparing and contrasting, agreeing and disagreeing respectfully, asserting ideas, cooperating, speaking clearly, listening carefully

Directions

1. Assign partners. Give each pair a sheet of paper, with directions for drawing a Venn diagram, or a diagram template.

2. Name the items that partners will compare and contrast. For example, "Compare and contrast tropical and temperate forests."

3. Give three to five minutes for partners to brainstorm ideas and write them in the appropriate place on the diagram.

4. Give a one-minute warning.

5. To share the work, each pair could share one thing they put in each section, or students could do a Museum Walk (p. 59).

Tips for Success

• Prepare sheets of paper or templates for each pair.

• Model how to brainstorm ideas and listen respectfully.

• Give examples of the kinds of things that could be written in each section of the diagram.

Classroom Snapshot

Venn Diagrams • "Today," Ms. Mayo tells the fourth graders, "you'll get to sharpen your ideas about how governments work by comparing and contrasting two forms: democracy and dictatorship."

Students pair up with their research partners and head to one of the large Venn diagrams taped to the wall. "You'll have three minutes to brainstorm similarities and differences of these two forms of government and write them on your diagram. Remember our rules for listening respectfully."

Margo and Theresa stand by their diagram. Margo starts: "In a democracy, we get to vote. Can people vote in a dictatorship?" They consult their textbook before writing "can vote" under democracy and "don't vote" under dictatorship.

Students get to move around a bit while reviewing and reflecting at the end of a lesson.

Skills practiced: Recalling key information from a lesson or unit of study, sharing ideas with others

Directions

1. Give each student a sheet with a three-by-three grid that asks them to note three specific kinds of reflections. For example, three categories might be "One thing I recall," "One thing I observed," and "My key insight."

2. Students mingle, find a partner, and exchange grids. Each fills in one box, initials it, and returns the grid.

3. At a signal, students find a new partner. Allow about one minute for each encounter.

4. Continue until students have filled in all nine boxes.

5. If time allows, ask a few volunteers to share one item from their grid.

Tips for Success

- Prepare the grids.
- Model safe movement.
- Give examples of the kinds of things that could be written in each square.
- Model finding a partner.

As students move into and out of small group conversations, they hear multiple perspectives on various topics.

Skills practiced: Listening, staying focused on a topic

Directions

1. Arrange the room like a café, with tables spread out and four to five chairs at each table. Put a card in the middle of each table naming a topic for discussion. Each table will have a different topic. For example, if you're studying the process of presidential elections in the United States, topics might include the electoral college, age requirements, term limits, and the ticket (president and vice president running together).

2. To begin, have students choose a table to sit at. Ask a focus question that could apply to all the topics. For example: "How does your piece of the presidential election process help it be a fair process?" Allow five minutes for discussion.

3. Signal to end the discussion and invite two or three people per table to change tables.

4. Ask a new focusing question or repeat the previous one. Everyone discusses with new tablemates.

5. At the end, one person from each table shares out a summary of the ideas discussed.

Tips for Success

• Set up tables with topic cards.

• Model safe movement.

• Model how to join a conversation.

• Model respectful listening.

• To be sure all voices are heard, consider providing a structure for small-group discussion, such as going around the table and each person saying one thing.

• Consider providing a note-taking sheet to help with summarizing ideas.

This is an adaptation of the World Café™, a structured conversational process, found at www.theworldcafe.com.

WRITTEN CONVERSATIONS

Students build on each other's ideas through written communication.

Skills practiced: Written reflection, responding to another's thoughts

Directions

1. Form groups of four to six students.

2. State a topic or pose a question. For example, in a unit of study on Earth's weather, you might ask, "What is one of the most destructive types of weather on Earth?"

3. Give students time to think and free-write in response to the question (two or three minutes).

4. At your signal, everyone passes their papers to the right. They then read and respond or add to the ideas.

5. Repeat until each paper returns to its original writer.

6. Share out a few ideas with the whole group.

Tips for Success

- Give examples of effective written responses to the focus question.

- Model writing respectful, thoughtful responses.

FINAL THOUGHT: LIGHT THE FIRE OF LEARNING

Interactive learning structures are fun—and that's no small thing. But even more importantly, they're purposeful. The learning structures presented in this chapter will get students moving, thinking, talking, sharing—engaging in their learning. Integrate these structures into your daily lessons and watch your class become a place where learning burns brightly for every child, every day.

Using Activities Kids Love

Third graders in Ms. Santoro's class have been learning about unit fractions. Midway through the unit, as a way to assess what they've learned so far, she has them create a "fraction museum." Working in groups of three, their task is to use clay, colored water in plastic cups, string, and paper strips to create a unit fraction display for the museum.

After Ms. Santoro gives the directions and models one idea for creating a display, the students gather in their triads and set to work. Lively conversation rings throughout the room as students divide up tasks and materials and make a plan for their work.

Kevin says, "If we roll the clay into a ball, we can flatten it out into a circle, like a pizza."

Andrea replies, "Oh yeah, and then we just have to divide it equally into four pieces and each 'slice' can represent one-fourth."

The group next to them overhears this plan, and Alexis exclaims, "Hey! If we do what the fourths group is doing and fold the paper strips once more like this, we have our display for one-eighth."

"And we can do the same thing with our clay, equally divide each piece in half and now we have eight equal pieces!" Isaiah concludes.

As they eagerly work with the materials, creative displays soon begin to appear.

Because children love to dance around, build things, get their hands dirty, and use their imaginations, lessons that incorporate movement, drama, art, and other creative activities really come alive for them.

With a small investment of time for planning and with proactive teaching, you can offer lessons that incorporate things kids love to do while still meeting rigorous learning goals. You'll find that students not only engage with and enjoy their learning, but are more willing to tackle challenging tasks and more likely to remember what they've learned.

> **Benefits of Incorporating Activities Students Love to Do**
>
> ➤ Makes lessons relevant for students
>
> ➤ Encourages students to tackle challenging tasks
>
> ➤ Provides the active participation that leads to increased learning

Some Considerations for Planning

In this chapter, you'll get lots of ideas for incorporating kid-friendly activities into daily lesson planning. A good place to start is with some questions to guide your planning.

✳ **How does the activity help students meet lesson goals?** Engaged learning is purposeful, so although we want activities to be enjoyable, we need to be sure they directly support our teaching goals. The activities we describe in this chapter can be used to meet a variety of teaching goals.

➤ **Do you want students to explore a new idea or learn new material?** Conducting an experiment, doing close observation, or building a model can energize and deepen their explorations.

➤ **Do you want them to practice a skill?** Consider building a practice session around a variety of manipulatives (dice, buttons, cards, blocks, etc.) that students can use in creative ways.

➤ **Do you want them to show what they've learned?** Activities that draw on movement, drama, music, writing, and art let children showcase their discoveries and growing skills.

✳ **Do the activities fit the needs and aptitudes of your class?** Consider what you know about students from your day-to-day observations (see Chapter 1).

➤ **Do most students seem to need physical activity and enjoy being active outside or in the gym, or do they prefer quieter activities?**

Knowing students' preferences helps you choose drama and movement activities that will engage them.

➤ **Do you have a chatty group that loves connecting with peers?** If so, plan for activities that let them collaborate with classmates.

➤ **How developed are students' motor skills?** For example, at nine and ten years old, students are still developing small motor skills; at eleven, these abilities are much more present. You'd therefore choose different art-based activities depending on students' ages.

✳ **How does the activity connect to students' interests and passions?** Listen carefully to children's sharing and conversation and draw on the interests and passions they mention when you choose activities. For example, most of my fourth grade students loved following our local sports teams, and they often enjoyed creating their own collections—rocks, seashells, stickers, erasers, key chains, and sports cards were popular. Sports scores found their way into math problems and writing prompts, and we'd use their collections to practice skills such as classification and organization. And when they shared about their passions with the class, they built and practiced key communication skills.

✳ **How does the activity or choice of activities address various learning styles?** Along with having a sense of the class's needs and aptitudes, it's important to note individual aptitudes and learning styles and provide a range of learning options throughout the day. For example, if children are demonstrating their understanding of a reading selection, choices could include writing and drawing as well as drama. Or in the course of a multi-day science unit, you could incorporate some writing and drawing along with movement and outdoors investigation.

F A Q • How will I find time to add in all these activities and still meet curriculum goals?

Remember that these activities are not add-ons or ways to give students a break from lessons. Rather, they're incorporated right into a lesson or practice session as the vehicle for students' learning. Scan through the activity ideas beginning on page 84 or take a look at the sample lessons in Chapters 5 and 6. You'll see how easily the activities can fit into your daily teaching and get a sense for which would work within your time constraints.

Consistently offering a variety of activities enables students to use their strengths and, with support, to risk trying new things and building new skills. (See Chapter 6 for more information on offering choices.)

Teach and practice how to do the activities

Although children love to do these activities, they don't necessarily know how to do them safely and productively. For activities to enhance learning, it's important that you first teach children how to do them in the context of the classroom. Interactive Modeling (Appendix B) is a great way to teach and practice routines and skills that students need to do in one particular way.

A third grade teacher prepares students for science observation

Third grade teacher Caltha Crowe planned a science lesson in which children would use hand lenses to observe baby caterpillars and then make notes about their observations. Students were excited about the opportunity to be scientists and do firsthand observation, but Ms. Crowe knew that both the lenses and the caterpillars could suffer if children didn't first learn about safe use and care of materials.

Before the lesson, she used Interactive Modeling to teach students how to take the lenses out of their cases, hold them safely, find the right focal length, and then put the lenses away. She also took time to model and practice how to safely handle the baby caterpillars. After having this up-front time to learn the basics, children set to work eagerly—and safely—on their scientific observations.

Use Interactive Modeling to teach academic skills as well

For the caterpillar observations, Ms. Crowe used Interactive Modeling to teach use and care of materials. Interactive Modeling is also a great strategy for teaching academic skills.

> ### Turn to Special Area Teachers for Ideas
>
> Art, music, and PE teachers are a wonderful source of ideas for activities to include in lessons. Are students making collages in art class? You could incorporate that as a choice in a lesson, perhaps as a way students can show what they've learned about a topic. Are they learning how to use rhythm instruments in music class? Perhaps you can integrate rhythmic counting into a math lesson.

For example, you can model how to:

* Give peer feedback
* Move safely during a pantomime activity
* Create and add ideas to a Venn diagram
* Read with a partner
* Do all the steps needed to make a diorama
* Listen to a podcast or other recording
* Conduct an interview

Once you've modeled the necessary skills, be sure to give students a chance to practice and then continue to observe as they put the skill into action. And remember to reinforce their positive efforts!

GUIDED DISCOVERY:
Explore Creative Ideas for Using Materials

Whereas Interactive Modeling is a way to teach students how to do something in one particular way, Guided Discovery is a strategy teachers can use to generate interest and excitement about classroom resources and help children explore many possible uses of these resources. Guided Discovery encourages students to offer ideas, act on them, and share the results of their work with others, which stimulates everyone's thinking about future uses of the material.

A Guided Discovery has five steps and usually takes about twenty minutes. It can be done at any time during the year but is usually used most frequently in the first weeks of school, when teachers introduce students to many of the materials they'll use throughout the year.

In the following pages you'll see an example of a Guided Discovery in a first grade classroom. Guided Discovery can be used in upper grades as well to help students think about new uses for familiar materials. (For a Guided Discovery Planning Guide, see Appendix C.)

Guided Discovery

Here are the five steps of a Guided Discovery, illustrated with an example from a first grade classroom

1. **Introduce the material and generate interest in it.**

   Ms. Wilson has gathered students in a circle. She points to the covered item in front of her and says, "Under here are some important math materials that we will work with in first grade."

   With children's curious eyes on her, she slowly reveals a set of tangrams and holds them up. "These are called tangrams. Who has seen these before?" Many of the students raise their hands.

2. **Brainstorm and demonstrate ideas for using the material to learn.**

   Ms. Wilson asks, "How do you think we could use these tangrams to help us learn?" As students call out ideas, Ms. Wilson makes a list on the board: "We could make pictures." "Trace shapes!" "Measure with them."

   She passes a few tangrams to Josh, asking him to show how he would use them for measuring. "Pay attention to what Josh does," she says. After he's done, she asks students what they noticed.

   "He took the ends of each tangram and put them together so they were touching," one student observes.

Other students demonstrate a few more ideas from the list.

3. **All students explore some of the ideas.**

   Ms. Wilson says, "You're now going to have ten minutes to try some of the ideas on our list. Each table has paper, pencils, and several sets of tangrams. You'll work individually but you can share ideas as you work." She sends the children off by table groups and they eagerly get busy.

   Ms. Wilson circulates, checking in with students, answering questions, and reinforcing their efforts. She pauses next to Abbie. "Abbie, are you tracing the shapes to make a picture?"

   "Yup," answers Abbie.

   Ms. Wilson continues, "Could you put two shapes together to create a new, larger shape that you could trace?"

   Abbie replies, "Um . . . I don't know. Let me see." She takes two shapes, puts them together, and then moves one around. Her face lights up. "I can use this to make a car!" she exclaims, and immediately begins tracing the shape onto her paper.

   Ms. Wilson sees Andrew struggling to trace a tangram. "Andrew, it can be hard to hold the shape and trace it.

Would you like an idea that could help?" He nods and Ms. Wilson shows him how to place a hand firmly on the tangram before starting to trace.

Ms. Wilson rings a chime to get children's attention. "You have two more minutes to finish what you're working on."

4. Students share their exploratory work.

Ms. Wilson rings the chime again. "You've all been working so hard and trying out lots of ideas. Now you'll get a chance to look at each other's work. Leave your work on the table and stand up.

"At my signal, walk quietly around the room and look at your classmates' work. Put your hands behind your backs so you aren't tempted to touch their creations. Look quietly and think to yourself about one new idea you get from looking at each other's work. You may begin now."

After a few minutes, she rings the chime and calls students to the circle. Once everyone is seated, she asks,

"Who would like to share a new idea you learned or saw?"

Ideas ring out: "I never knew you could stack tangrams." "I saw how you could put shapes together to make new shapes." "Abbie made a car!"

5. Guide cleanup and care of materials.

"It sounds like you've all got lots of ideas," Ms. Wilson says. "We'll store the tangrams in bags so they are in complete sets and put them on the math shelf. Nicolai, can you show us how to put the tangrams away and return them to the math shelf? Watch what Nicolai does."

Nicolai goes to his workspace, carefully stacks a set of tangrams, slips them into their bag, and then carries the bag to the math shelf.

After students voice what they noticed, Ms. Wilson says, "We'll use the tangrams during math class. You can also use them independently during indoor recess and quiet time."

Things Kids Love To Do

In this section you'll find a wealth of kid-friendly ideas that will bring lessons to life.

Move, play, act, and perform

Kids love dramatic play and movement. Think back to your own childhood. Perhaps you had a suitcase full of old clothes for dress-up, got together with friends to act out imagined scenes, made up plays for dolls, or saved the day with action figures. You can build on students' passion for movement and drama to help them engage with learning in a range of subject areas.

Skills gained and practiced through these types of activities include collaboration, interpretation, creativity, presentation, public speaking, acting, dramatization, creative movement, storytelling, and spatial awareness.

Pantomime; dress up; create a living freeze frame or tableau

* **K–2:** The teacher narrates a story and students act it out. For example, the teacher might read a story about how an apple seed grows into a tree and students would each act out the process as the teacher reads.

F A Q • Does incorporating movement and drama mean we're putting on performances? That will take a lot of time.

Incorporating movement and drama doesn't need to lead to a big production. In fact, to keep these activities low-risk and focused on learning, any performance or sharing of work should be informal, with classmates as audience—not the entire school community.

* **3–6:** Students research a famous person, dress up like the person, and give a short speech as if they are that person.

Put on a puppet show; write and perform a skit or play; create a video

* **K–2:** Students use puppets to retell a familiar story. The focus could be on order of events, patterns in a story, dialogue, or alternative endings.

* **3–6:** Students work in pairs or small groups to write, create, and record a video; for example, they might make a video about a recently read book or a presentation of research results.

* **3–6:** In small groups, students create and act out math word problems.

Classroom Snapshot

Fifth graders in Mrs. Bousquet's classroom worked with partners to write, perform, and videotape a commercial for a favorite book they'd read during the year. Each pair chose a book and then developed ideas for the commercial, wrote jingles or songs, and came up with persuasive language to use. At the end of the project, students shared their videos. Classmates wrote on a slip of paper one reason they might choose to read the book and handed the paper to the presenting pair.

Create a dance

* **K–2:** Students use dance movements to dramatize events in a story.

* **3–6:** Students use movement to demonstrate different systems of the body, such as the circulatory system.

Write and sing a song or jingle; create and perform a rhythm; create a chant, cheer, or rap

* **K–2:** Students create a cheer to explain a scientific process. For example, students can cheer for a bean seed as it grows into a plant or a water drop as it travels through the water cycle.

* **3–6:** Individual students create a rap to help learn hard-to-remember math facts.

* **K–6:** Students tap out the rhythmic pattern in a poem.

Observe, research, and collect

Children are naturally curious, always investigating and interacting with the world around them. Watch a child walking through the woods or down a neighborhood street or just exploring the backyard. They seem to have a built-in desire to make sense of their environment and often find joy in the smallest of discoveries. They love to ask questions, find out how things work, and spend time outside in nature. They adore animals of all kinds and enjoy collecting things. You can nurture this innate curiosity by giving them time for exploration, observation, and research.

Along with observation, skills gained and practiced through these types of activities include measuring, classifying, predicting, interpreting, recording, and communicating.

Do a science experiment or demonstration

✳ **3–6:** Students go through all the steps of setting up and conducting an experiment—developing a testable question, brainstorming hypotheses, writing procedures, collecting and analyzing data, and writing a conclusion.

Create a garden or plant seeds—inside or outside

✳ **K–2:** Students germinate and plant seeds in an indoor garden or create and tend an outdoor garden.

✳ **3–6:** To plan a vegetable garden, students research which plants are best for the climate where they live, how and when to plant each variety, and what's needed to care for them. Older students could even work within a budget and plan for needed supplies. The vegetables they grow could be used for a class meal that students help cook or donated to a local food pantry.

Collect or catch leaves, rocks, bugs, sticks

✳ **K–2:** As part of a study of seeds and how they travel, students create seed collections. In pairs, they collect seeds and then sort and label them.

✳ **3–6:** In small groups, students collect rocks and then sort and classify their collections.

✳ **3–6:** Students collect leaves from trees near their school or at a nearby park and identify the types of trees the leaves came from. The class then creates "tree maps" in which the location and type of each tree in a designated area is labeled; they use the leaves on the map as part of the labels.

Study a map or globe; study a picture (painting, photograph, illustration, etc.)

✳ **K–6:** At the start of an art class, students look closely at several works of impressionist art; then they brainstorm words that describe this style of painting.

* **K–6:** In PE, students study a world map labeled with the most popular sports in each country or region and then choose one to play.

* **3–6:** Students study maps of the early American colonies to determine why leaders decided to settle in those areas and not others.

Classroom Snapshot

In Jane Cofie-Raczko's first grade classroom, students study birds as part of the science curriculum. A bird feeder hangs right outside the classroom window. Students observe the types of birds that visit the feeder at various times each day and record observations in a field journal. Students are very engaged with this lesson and their observations continue throughout the day, including during recess when birds fly overhead or stop and perch on the playground equipment.

Observe an object (with naked eye, microscope, magnifying lens, etc.) and record observations

* **K–2:** Students germinate seeds and observe changes in the seeds over time. Using drawings and words, they note changes in a journal.

* **K–6:** Students collect insects in clear containers and observe them for several minutes as they make sketches and write observations in science journals.

* **3–6:** Students observe, chart, and illustrate the phases of the moon and describe the orbital motion of the moon as it revolves around Earth.

Conduct research using various sources such as textbooks, reference books, and online resources

* **K–2:** Students choose an animal to research through early reader books. They look for information on what the animal looks like, what it eats, and where it lives.

* **3–6:** Working in small groups, students explore a topic by doing a Web Quest. Each group has its own research question, and each member has a specific role such as facilitator, recorder, or timekeeper.

Sculpt, build, and create

Children love to construct, build, sculpt, draw, and color. They begin with visions of what they might create and then dive in, solving problems and adjusting and refining their ideas as they go. By supporting and encouraging their explorations, you can help them develop resilience and persistence and learn to love the process as well as the finished product.

Skills gained and practiced through these types of activities include problem-solving, engineering, designing, drafting, assembling, building, using supplies creatively and responsibly, recreating physical objects or structures on a smaller scale, and learning from mistakes.

Build models with clay, scavenged or recycled materials, papier-mâché, etc.

* **K–6:** Build a model of a molecule, Native American home, insect, setting of a story, the solar system, etc.

Create a museum display

* **K–6:** Students sort, label, and display a range of items—fossils or ancient Egyptian artifacts they've recreated, rock and mineral collections, leaves. Creating museum displays often goes hand in hand with activities that involve collecting (see pages 85–86).

* **K–6:** Students create displays of habitats, dinosaurs, or book settings.

Create a board game

* **3–6:** Students create a game around a series of important events in a specific time in history (Civil War, Industrial Revolution, etc.) or the important events in a story or book.

Create an illustration by drawing, painting, using rubber stamps and ink, or creating a collage or mural

* **K–2:** With clip art, students create collages of animals found in various habitats.

* **3–6:** Students share what they've learned about weather by creating murals depicting the types of weather found in different regions of the United States.

Classroom Snapshot

In Ms. Jacoby's third grade classroom, students have been learning about simple machines. Toward the end of the unit, they focus on the pulley. Working in small groups, their task is to use objects such as a block of wood, string, washers, etc., to create a pulley that can lift small weights off the ground.

For most students, the school flagpole serves as their only reference point for understanding how a pulley works. With this knowledge, along with their knowledge of other simple machines, they set energetically to work.

Communicate and share

School-age children love to share with others what they know and what they're thinking about. Nurturing this passion serves them well because strong speaking and listening skills are essential for school success.

Skills gained and practiced through these activities include reading, writing, public speaking, listening, discussion, computer skills, observation, debate, and turn-taking.

Listen to a speech, lecture, podcast, or radio show; watch a video clip or DVD

* **K–6:** Listen to Martin Luther King, Jr.'s "I Have a Dream" speech or the Gettysburg Address and talk with a partner about a personal connection they make to the speech.

Participate in a discussion

* **K–6:** Students form clubs or circles in which they discuss literature, science, math, or any other content area they especially enjoy.

Write a magazine or newspaper article

* **3–6:** Students write an article that might have appeared in a newspaper at a specific time in history or write about current events at school.

Create riddles

* **K–6:** Students write riddles for others to solve about famous people, vocabulary, science facts, etc.

Write a letter or story

* **K–6:** Students write letters from the point of view of famous people in history, story characters, or world leaders; or they write one story from various points of view.

Create a poster, brochure, or slide show

* **K–2:** Students create a poster to show how a story character might have been feeling during a specific moment in the story.

* **3–6:** To present information learned during a research project, students create a slide show, website, or series of blog posts.

At the end of the year, Claudia Shultz's second grade class does a unit on Goods and Services. One year, as part of this unit, students worked in small groups to interview various school employees about their jobs. They followed a three-step process: 1) preparing for the interview, 2) doing the interview itself, and 3) writing a short news article to share what they learned in the interview.

Plan and conduct an interview either in person or on the phone

✳ **K–6:** Students use interviews with knowledgeable people to gather information for a research project; interview community members to learn about their city or town; or invite artists, scientists, engineers, etc., for a Q&A session about their work.

Take part in a debate; write a persuasive essay or paragraph

✳ **K–2:** Students assume the roles of various storybook characters and debate from their points of view.

✳ **3–6:** Students write persuasive essays to school or town leaders advocating for changes they think might benefit the school or community.

Create a script for a radio show or podcast; write and deliver a speech; write and deliver a monologue

✳ **K–6:** Students create and present a speech as if they were a famous person in history or a story character.

✳ **3–6:** Students create their own podcasts to share facts they've discovered in their research, their views on environmental issues, etc.

Write a poem or a story; write a memoir; write a blog post, journal, diary entry

✳ **K–2:** Students create shape poems about animals they've studied.

✳ **3–6:** Students write diary entries as if they are characters living during a specific time or event in history.

Write instructions or "how to" manual

* **K–6:** Students create "how to" books based on science topics, such as "How to grow into a plant from a seed" or "How to form a planet."

* **3–6:** Students create directions for various academic procedures, such as math computations or editing.

Create a comic strip

* **3–6:** Students create comic strips to share their understanding of equivalent fractions, decimals, percents, or other math concepts.

FINAL THOUGHT: MAKE LEARNING SPARKLE

The more students can approach learning in a spirit of play and exploration, the more invested they'll be, even during challenging work. Incorporate some of the ideas in this chapter into daily lessons and watch students become enthusiastic participants in classroom life!

Structuring Lessons for Maximum Impact

Second grade teacher Ms. Stephanis is beginning a unit on personal narrative writing. To open the first lesson, she gathers students in the meeting circle and begins to read aloud *Owl Moon* by Jane Yolen.

"It was late one winter night, long past my bedtime, when Pa and I went owling," she reads. The students listen raptly, all eyes on the book that Ms. Stephanis holds up. When she finishes reading, she pauses for a moment to let students sit with the story.

"Looked like you were all caught up in that adventure!" she says. "I know I was. That story is called a personal narrative, and for the next few weeks, you will be authors and illustrators of your own personal narratives. You'll be writing your own stories about events from your lives. You'll learn how to use words to paint a picture in your reader's mind, like Jane Yolen did for us. Today, we're going to spend some time talking about what makes a story really come to life. Then you're going to start thinking about your own stories and how you can paint a picture through writing.

"Now let's think: What parts of this story made you feel as if you were right there in the forest with the girl and her father? What words did the author use to bring this story to life? Turn to an elbow partner and share your ideas."

Students quickly turn to a partner and begin to share examples from the story. After a few minutes, Ms. Stephanis raises her hand for quiet. Students finish speaking and look at her.

She picks up a marker and says, "Let's start a list of the parts of this book that grabbed our attention. Raise your hand if you have an idea to share."

This lesson opening took only a few minutes, but a lot happened in that time. The reading and partner chat captured students' attention and helped them make a personal connection to the idea of narrative writing. Students' senses were engaged—they heard imaginative use of language and saw evocative illustrations. And their minds were engaged as they thought and talked about how this piece of writing pulled them in.

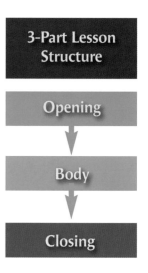

In the days to come, students will write their stories using colorful details and other strategies to stir readers' hearts and minds. They will learn about narrative sequencing, voice, and tone, and they'll gain appreciation of both the challenges and the joys of writing.

In this chapter, you'll learn about a three-part lesson structure of opening, body, and closing that will help you plan lessons that heighten students' engagement and deepen their learning.

Benefits of the Three-Part Lesson Structure

➤ Reflects the natural learning cycle

➤ Provides a structure for helping students make a personal connection to their learning at the beginning of the lesson

➤ Provides time for reflecting on learning at the end

➤ Sets an effective pace for learning

The Ideal Lesson Structure

The three-part structure reflects the natural learning cycle we presented in the introduction. It's effective for lessons of any length and for any age group.

In the midst of a busy teaching day, it can be tempting to do only the body of the lesson—the working-with-content part—and skip the opening and closing. I often did that in my early days in teaching. But I soon learned that taking the time to open and close the lesson in an orderly, inviting way helped students connect more deeply with the content and feel more invested in their work.

1. Opening: What will I learn? Why does it matter?

Engaged learning is purposeful. At the start of a lesson, students need to hear why they're reading about pioneers moving west or learning a new math strategy or practicing vocabulary words.

Engaged learning is also connected to students' lives: their interests, strengths, and stores of knowledge. What do students already know about this topic? What do they want to know? How does the topic connect to their daily lives? How will it help them grow as learners?

Opening		
Purpose	**Teacher's role**	**Looks and sounds like . . .**

• To intrigue, excite, and motivate students about the lesson	• Say what students will be learning in this lesson and why it matters
	
	• Help students make a personal connection to this learning
	
	• Give directions for the tasks students will be doing (or give directions in the body of the lesson)
		• Teacher using envisioning language and open-ended questions
		
		• Students sharing ideas through:
		  – a whole-group, teacher-facilitated conversation
		  – partner chatting
		  – an interactive learning structure

Teacher's role in the opening of a lesson

During the opening of any lesson, the teacher needs to set a positive tone for learning. The opening might be as simple as gathering all the students in a circle and having a conversation with them in which you name the purpose and give directions for the lesson, or it might include opportunities for children to talk with each other or engage with content material in some way. No matter how simple or complex the opening, the way you structure the interactions and the language you use can go a long way toward increasing students' engagement during the body of the lesson.

Use envisioning language and open-ended questions. Think back to the opening vignette. Ms. Stephanis could have simply said, "We've been reading personal narratives and today we're going to begin writing our own stories. Here are some elements of a personal narrative." These words would have named the purpose and set a direction but they wouldn't have necessarily excited children's imaginations.

Instead, after showing a vivid example of personal narrative, Ms. Stephanis used envisioning language ("You'll be writing your own stories about events from your lives. You'll learn how to use words to paint a picture in your reader's mind, like Jane Yolen did for us") to pull children in. She also used open-ended questions ("What parts of this story made you feel like you were right there in the forest?") to get them actively thinking about and responding to the story. This language gave students a compelling identity—they'll be authors and illustrators, writing stories that paint a picture! It also helped them think about what they'd observed about narrative writing and begin to build their "how-to" knowledge. (See Appendix A for information about envisioning language and open-ended questions.)

Use interactive learning structures. You can use an interactive learning structure to help children talk with classmates and make an initial connection to the topic. For example, to help students access prior knowledge, you could have them chat with an elbow partner, as Ms. Stephanis did, or you could use a structure such as Mix and Mingle to Music (p. 58) to have them talk with a variety of partners. If you want children to take a position on a topic, you could use a structure such as Four Corners (p. 53).

Pay attention to transitions. As you plan the lesson, think about what the transitions will be from the opening to the body of the lesson. Will children need to move from a whole group circle to individual work spaces? Will they be working with partners or small groups? Plan in advance how children can most smoothly make this shift and use Interactive Modeling as needed to teach routines such as getting materials, moving chairs and tables, or finding a partner to work with.

2. Body: How can I best learn this?

The body of the lesson is where the six characteristics of engaging academics you learned about in the introduction come into play. For students to truly connect with the lesson, the work they do needs to be:

* Active

* Interactive

* Purposeful

* Appropriately challenging

* Connected to their interests

* Structured with opportunities for autonomy

Although you might include some direct teaching in the body, this is also a time for students to move beyond listening and absorbing. They need opportunities to practice, to explore and experiment, to ask questions and look for answers, to learn on their own and with peers, and to make personal meaning out of the information they take in.

In planning the body of a lesson, you can draw on strategies presented in this book. You might consider:

* How to make use of your knowledge of students to best address their learning needs (Chapter 1)

* How to group students in a way that will help them all do their best learning (Chapter 2)

* What language of learning skills to highlight (pp. 32–36)

✳ What kinds of interactive learning structures to use (Chapter 3)

✳ How to incorporate activities that students are naturally drawn to (Chapter 4)

✳ What teacher-guided choices you might offer (Chapter 6)

Body		
Purpose	**Teacher's role**	**Looks and sounds like . . .**
• Students dig into the work, trying out ideas, practicing skills, researching, absorbing, and applying new learning	• Observe students at work • Facilitate students' work • Coach as needed	• Teacher using open-ended questions and reinforcing language • Students working independently on active and interactive tasks

Teacher's role in the body of the lesson

Although you might do a small amount of direct teaching with the whole class, your primary role during the body of the lesson will be to observe, facilitate, and coach. How much time you spend on each will depend on students' ability to work collaboratively and independently.

The balance of these roles will shift from lesson to lesson—at times where there's a smooth hum of independent activity, you might primarily observe, facilitate, and reinforce the positive things you see happening. At other times you'll be more actively involved with coaching individuals and small groups.

Observe. In your daily observations of students, you'll learn a lot about how their abilities and skills are evolving, how their interests are shifting, how well they understand various concepts, and how adept they are at social interactions.

You'll note who is able to sustain focus and who is easily distracted; which students are eager and which are having a hard time getting started; who seems frustrated and who seems to be enjoying the work; and whether some students struggle to remember simple instructions while others help classmates remember what needs to be done. These observations will guide interventions during the lesson as well as future planning.

Facilitate and coach. From your observations, you'll learn when you can best support students by stepping in to facilitate and coach as they work. The goals of facilitating and coaching are to:

* Keep students on topic
* Help them work through stuck points
* Correct any misunderstandings about content or process
* Support effective collaboration
* Help students stretch themselves

Use open-ended questions. Open-ended questions are those which have no single right or wrong answer. Instead, any reasoned answer is a good one. Asking open-ended questions such as "What might you do next?" or "How do you plan to finish this task?" can help guide students while allowing them to stay in charge of their work.

When asking open-ended questions, it's important that you genuinely want to know the student's thinking. If you ask a question with a "correct" answer in mind, students will catch on that you really aren't asking for their ideas. For example, if you ask, "Why did you use this color?" be open to considering the student's reason rather than looking for the student to say, "Yeah, I probably should've used blue instead."

If you think a suggestion is needed, it's best to give it directly rather than framing it as a question. For example, "We agreed that we'd use blue to represent group A in this graph. So I think you should color that bar blue."

Also, avoid using pseudo open-ended questions, such as "What should you be doing right now?" to redirect a student who is clearly off task. Instead, just tell them what to do. "Danny, put away your backpack and work on your cityscape."

Ask first before offering direction or help. If coaching is going to be truly useful, students need to want our help. We might have all sorts of great ideas about a student's work—but we need to remember that it is the student's work, not ours.

Before offering advice or suggestions, pause for a moment; then ask, "Would you like some help with that?" or "Can I offer a suggestion that has helped other fourth grade students?" If the student says, "Yes," then proceed with a guiding question or a suggestion.

But if a student says, "No, not right now," you need to honor that, step back, and continue to observe the student's work. Check in periodically to see how things are progressing. If the work is appropriately challenging, the student can learn a lot from working through problems independently.

When providing instruction, keep it brief and focused. In situations where students welcome your help, keep the guidance brief and focused to help them retain a sense of ownership of their work. You might offer help doing a particular task. For example, if a student is having a hard time looking through a hand lens you could help them find the right focal distance. Or you might give feedback that embeds key vocabulary words, for example, "You've made a trapezoid—see how it has four sides? That makes it a trapezoid."

Check in with all students at some point. Even students who are working well at their task need your attention. This is a great time to use reinforcing language to acknowledge something they've achieved or to underscore their work process; for example, you might say, "I see you have moved on to edit your friendly letter" or "This timeline clearly shows all the important events in Martin Luther King, Jr.'s, life."

Teach and reteach skills

If a large number of students need help, it might be time to reassess students' skills and comfort with routines. Do you need to reteach some academic skills? Simplify tasks? Are problems arising from students' working in groups? If so, do you need to have them work independently until you've retaught key collaborative skills (pp. 32–36)?

An abbreviated Interactive Modeling is a great strategy to use to revisit both academic and logistical tasks. For example, if students are struggling with careful use of markers, you could ring the chime to get their attention and then briefly say, "I've noticed that many of you are forgetting to put the caps back on markers or are putting the caps on too loosely. This means the markers are drying out. Watch how I put the cap on."

Demonstrate how to put the cap on tightly and ask for students' observations. Make sure to mention that they should hear a "snap" when the cap is on tightly. Finally, have all students practice putting the cap on a marker, making sure they hear the "snap."

Pay attention to transitions

As with moving from the opening of the lesson to the body, you'll want to plan for transitions from the body to the closing section.

Have students been intently focused on a task? Perhaps you'll want to get the blood and oxygen flowing with a quick movement break such as yoga stretching or a quick round of Head, Shoulders, Knees, and Toes. Do students need to move from table groups or individual work spaces to the circle area? Be sure you've modeled and practiced how to do so quickly, quietly, and efficiently. If students need to bring finished work products with them or display the products somewhere, clearly indicate where the products should go and model how to care for them in transit.

3. Closing: What did I learn? What might I do next time?

During the closing of a lesson, students assimilate and consolidate what they've learned. In a short lesson, this might consist of a quick restatement of the purpose of the lesson and a summary of what was practiced or learned.

This is also a time when students can reflect on their learning, gaining more understanding about themselves as learners while deepening their mastery of academic content. Thinking and talking about work can also provide a sense of closure that makes it easier for students to disengage from the task and move on to another topic or activity.

Closing		
Purpose	**Teacher's role**	**Looks and sounds like . . .**
• Students assimilate and consolidate what they've learned	• Summarize what was practiced or learned • Facilitate reflection • Make connections to other learning	• Teacher using open-ended questions and reinforcing language • Students reflecting individually, with a partner or small group, or in the large group

Teacher's role in the closing of the lesson

In the closing segment, the teacher provides a way for students to reflect on their learning and the activities they were engaged with and to consider how these met the purpose of the lesson. During closing, you might summarize the lesson or help students summarize, make connections to other learning, and reflect or share about their learning.

Use open-ended questions to facilitate reflection

One of the best ways to stimulate reflection is to ask open-ended questions. In the lesson from the opening vignette, Ms. Stephanis might ask a question such as "What's one thing you learned about narrative story writing that you want to remember to use when you write your own story?"

In a math class, a teacher might ask, "What worked well in this review of math facts? What would you do differently the next time you practice these math facts?" Questions such as these help students consider how their own actions influence the outcomes of their work.

You can also ask questions that encourage children to learn from each other, for example, "What is one new idea you got from looking at your classmates' maps?"

Sample Lesson Plans

In the following pages, you'll find sample lesson plans at both the primary and upper elementary levels. These lessons show how to use an opening, body, and closing to meet lesson objectives in ways that engage children and deepen their learning.

Each lesson draws on strategies presented in this book and we've provided icons to help you quickly identify these strategies:

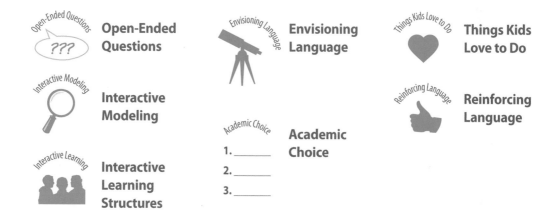

Open-Ended Questions

Interactive Modeling

Interactive Learning Structures

Envisioning Language

Academic Choice

Things Kids Love to Do

Reinforcing Language

Use the sample plans to inspire your own lesson planning. In Appendix C, you'll find a Lesson Planning Guide template with questions to guide your thinking.

Retelling a Story

How many times have you heard a good story and wanted to retell it? The first step is remembering the details—a skill students can learn and practice as early as kindergarten.

In this lesson, students get to practice retelling a familiar story using important details. They begin by talking with classmates, helping each other remember key elements of the story. Then they choose one of four ways to retell the story.

Lesson goal/purpose: Students will practice the skill of retelling a familiar story using important details from the text.

CCSS/curriculum standard: CCSS.ELA-LITERACY.RL.K.3: With prompting and support, identify characters, settings, and major events in a story.

Time needed: 40 minutes

Materials:

- Book or story that students are very familiar with (they've read it themselves or heard it read aloud many times already)

- Instrumental music to play during the Mix and Mingle to Music activity—choose music that will be lively but not distracting

- Art supplies such as crayons, colored pencils, pencils

- Large sheets of paper divided into six sections

- Premade sets of story character stick puppets

PROCEDURE

Opening ✳ 15 Minutes

Envisioning Language

1. **Gather students together in a circle and name the goal for the lesson:**

   "Have you ever heard a really good story and wanted to tell it to someone else? Today you're going to practice retelling a story. To retell a story you have to pay attention and remember details. Being able to do this will also help you out when you start reading longer stories and chapter books."

   Show students the book or story they'll be working with for this lesson. Remind them that they know this story well and tell them they're going to do an activity that will help them remember all the details. (If needed, read the story aloud again.)

2. **Give directions for Mix and Mingle to Music (p. 58).** Students move around the room while music plays. When the music stops, they find a partner and each briefly answers a teacher-posed question, such as:

   Interactive Learning

   Who are the main characters in this story?

   Where does the story take place?

   What is the first important event in this story?

   What is the big problem in this story?

   How does the story end?

3. End the activity and have students return to the circle. Describe the choices they'll have for retelling the story. Let them know that they need to include six important details from the story, in order. The choices to retell the story are:

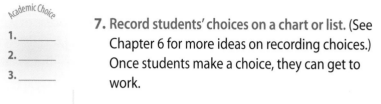

Academic Choice

1. _____
2. _____
3. _____

Art · Draw six important details from the book, using paper already divided into six parts.

Writing · Write about six important details from the book, using either the paper already divided into six parts or lined paper.

Drama · Use the stick puppets to act out six important details from the book.

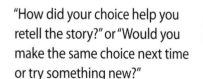

Things Kids Love to Do

Movement · Use your body to act out six important details from the book.

4. Help students make good choices. Briefly brainstorm, "Why might someone choose writing? Why might someone choose movement?"

5. Remind students of any special rules about using any of the materials. For example: "Remember to hold the stick puppets lightly." Use Interactive Modeling as needed to prepare students for these choices.

Interactive Modeling

6. Let them know where they can find and gather materials and where they can do their work (at specific tables, on the floor, special area of the classroom, etc.).

7. Record students' choices on a chart or list. (See Chapter 6 for more ideas on recording choices.) Once students make a choice, they can get to work.

Body ✳ 20 Minutes

1. Students gather materials and begin working, creating, and practicing. Circulate while they work to help them stay on task and to answer questions.

2. As students finish with their work, pair them up so they can share their work with each other.

Closing ✳ 5 Minutes

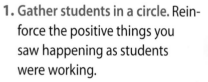

1. Gather students in a circle. Reinforce the positive things you saw happening as students were working.

Reinforcing Language

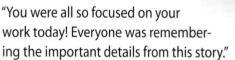

"You were all so focused on your work today! Everyone was remembering the important details from this story."

2. Ask a few reflection questions. Students share their answers with a partner or with the whole group.

"How did your choice help you retell the story?" or "Would you make the same choice next time or try something new?"

Open-Ended Questions

???

Graphing

The process of gathering data and transforming it into a graph calls on a range of skills and aptitudes used in many disciplines—and it's fun!

Lesson goal/purpose: Practice creating a bar graph from a set of data; create and solve problems based on the data represented in the graph.

CCSS/curriculum standard: CCSS.MATH.CONTENT.2.MD.10: Draw a picture graph and a bar graph (with single-unit scale) to represent a data set with up to four categories. Solve simple put-together, take-apart, and compare problems using information presented in a bar graph.

Time needed: 60 minutes

Materials: One-inch graph paper, markers, rulers, paper, and pencils

PROCEDURE

Opening ✳ 15 Minutes

1. **Gather students together in a circle near a whiteboard or chart paper. Share the purpose of the lesson:**

   "Last week we started learning about bar graphs. Today's lesson will help you practice creating, reading, and using graphs. We need to know how to figure out what information graphs are communicating to us and how we can use that information. For example, today we're going to use a graph to show our thoughts about fun recess activities."

   Show examples of graphs from a newspaper, magazine, and/ or website and share how you might use one of the graphs. Ask students to think and talk about how graphing the data in the example might help them use the information.

2. **Let students know that as a class, you are going to collect and graph some data about their favorite recess activity:** the swings, the climbing structure, hard-top games (such as basketball or four-square), or field games (such as soccer or tag).

3. **On chart paper or a whiteboard, create a simple chart to collect the data. For example:**

   Favorite Recess Activity:

   Swings _____

   Climbing structure _____

   Hard-top games _____

   Field games _____

4. **Use the interactive learning structure Four Corners (p. 53) to collect the data.** Label each corner of the room with one of the recess choices. Have students move to the corner of the room that represents their favorite recess activity. Ask each corner to report out how many students made that choice. Record the number of students for each recess activity on the chart you created.

Interactive Learning

Body ✳ 30–40 Minutes

1. **Have an example of a bar graph to share as a model.** Ask students to remember the important characteristics of a bar graph that they learned in an earlier lesson. Use an anchor chart with characteristics of bar graphs as a visual reminder for students. For example:

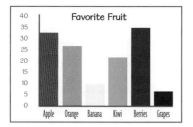

All graphs have:
- A title
- Labels
- Scales
- Bars of equal width
- Optional: different colors for each bar

2. **Tell students they'll have about fifteen minutes** (adjust as needed for your students and schedule) to create their own individual bar graph representing the data just collected about favorite recess activities. Have students move to tables or desks where graph paper, rulers, and markers are available.

Things Kids Love to Do

3. **Circulate** and make sure students are representing the data accurately and that each graph has the required characteristics.

4. **Have students bring their graphs and form concentric circles. Do Inside-Outside Circles (p. 55) to work with the data on the graphs they just created.**

Interactive Learning

a. When everyone is standing across from a partner, pose a question or math problem. Partners use their graphs to help them find the answer. Then have the outside circle move to create new partnerships and ask a new question or present a new problem to solve.

b. Sample questions: How many more children chose field games than swings? • How many students chose hard-top games and climbing structure as their favorite recess activity? • What recess activity was the least popular?

Closing ✳ 5–10 Minutes

1. **Ask a focus question** to help students summarize learning. "Looking at our graphs, what have we learned about favorite recess activities?"

Open-Ended Questions
???

2. **Use Maître d' (p. 57) for reflection:**

a. Table for 4—one thing I like about the graph I created

Interactive Learning

b. Table for 3—one math problem I thought was challenging to solve

c. Table for 2—one way I worked well with a partner

Classifying & Identifying Rocks

Lesson goal/purpose: Students will organize rocks by properties they can observe.

Next Generation Science Standards/curriculum standard: 5-PS1-3 for grades 3–5: Make observations and measurements to identify materials based on their properties.

Time needed: 50 minutes

Materials:

- Various samples of rocks (these could be provided by the teacher, collected by students, or a combination of both)

- Chart paper

- Markers

- Hand lenses

Children, especially between the ages of eight and ten, could be museum curators—they love to collect things, sort them, display them, and share their collections with friends. This lesson calls on that interest as students organize and display rocks they've collected in an earlier lesson.

P R O C E D U R E

Opening ✳ 10 Minutes

1. Gather students in a circle and name the purposes of the lesson:

   Envisioning Language

   "Today you will be organizing a variety of rocks by using what you can see and observe. This will help you learn important characteristics that rocks have and begin to learn how to identify rocks. You will also be practicing important skills that scientists use— careful observation and classification."

2. Display a blank K-W-L chart titled "Rocks." Ask students, "What do you know about rocks?" First have them talk with a partner and then ask for ideas to put in the K column.

Rocks		
Know	Want to know	Learned

3. Ask, "What do you want to learn about rocks?" Students talk first with their partners and then share ideas that you write in the W column. Let students know that they will add some ideas to the L column after the lesson today.

Open-Ended Questions

???

4. Brainstorm observable properties of rocks—give a couple of examples if necessary. Post this list where students can easily refer to it as they work. For example, the list might include:

Color	Weight
Texture	Has layers
Makes marks on paper	Size

Body ✳ 20 Minutes

1. Divide students into groups of three or four and have them move to designated work spaces.

2. Prepare students for productive collaborative work. One way to do this is to refer to class rules:

"When we work with others in this lesson, what class rule will be important to follow so we can accomplish our task today? What might that look like and sound like?"

3. Give each group a piece of chart paper, some markers, a few hand lenses, and the rock samples.

4. Give directions for the activity orally, one step at a time.

Things Kids Love to Do

a. "Place all the rock samples in a pile at the top of the paper and draw a circle around the pile of rocks.

b. Move all the dark-colored rocks into a pile on one side of the chart paper under the circle. Draw a circle around them. Label this pile as 'dark.'

c. Move all the light-colored rocks into a pile on the other side of the chart paper under the circle. Draw a circle around this pile. Label this pile as 'light.' You should now have two piles.

d. Focus on one of these piles of rocks. Choose a physical property that will allow you to divide these rocks into two more categories. Refer to the list that you brainstormed. For example, if you decide to categorize the rocks by texture, you could divide them into a 'rough' pile and a 'smooth' pile.

e. Sort your dark and light piles according to the new categories you've chosen. Then draw a circle around each of those piles and label it. You should now have four piles.

f. Can you divide each of the piles one more time by using new characteristics? You will then have eight piles." (If necessary, give an example, such as categorizing the rocks by size and dividing the piles into a "large" pile and a "small" pile.)

5. Direct students to leave the chart papers in the centers of their tables. Do a Museum Walk (p. 59) so students can look at class-mates' charts.

Interactive Learning

6. Create a classroom rock museum display: From the piles on the chart paper, each student chooses one rock to describe us-ing at least three characteristics (for example: dark, has more than two colors, heavy).

Academic Choice

1. _____
2. _____
3. _____

7. Each student creates a label for their chosen rock by folding a notecard so it can stand up and writing the characteristics of the rock on one side of the notecard so someone else can easily read it.

8. Place the rocks and labels together some-where in the classroom where everyone can see them (on a table, on top of a bookshelf, on a window ledge).

9. Finish the K-W-L chart by seeing if any knowledge in the K column was confirmed and if any ques-tions in the W column were answered. Add new questions that have come up in the W column, and add some new learning about rocks to the L column.

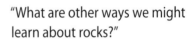
Open-Ended Questions
???

Closing ✳ 10 Minutes

Interactive Learning

Use the Inside-Outside Circles structure (p. 55) to help students share reflections on their learning. As students rotate to new partners, ask questions such as:

"What was easy about this task? What was hard?"

"What are other ways we might learn about rocks?"

Open-Ended Questions
???

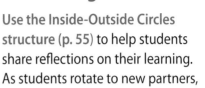

Debate

Lesson goal/purpose: Students will conduct research and practice using evidence in a debate.

CCSS/curriculum standard: CCSS.ELA-LITERACY.SL.6.4: Present claims and findings, sequencing ideas logically and using pertinent descriptions, facts, and details to accentuate main ideas or themes; use appropriate eye contact, adequate volume, and clear pronunciation.

CCSS.ELA-LITERACY.SL.6.5: Include multimedia components (e.g., graphics, images, music, sound) and visual displays in presentations to clarify information.

Time needed: About 90 minutes; can be spread out over two class periods (opening and research in one class period, creation of presentations and performances along with the closing in another class period).

Materials:

- Art supplies

- Access to the Internet

- Books

lder students enjoy debating various sides of issues. This lesson incorporates the practice and use of many life skills, including gathering facts and data, looking at an issue from multiple viewpoints, and debating by using evidence and carefully crafted arguments.

PROCEDURE

Opening ✳ 10–15 Minutes

1. Share the purpose of the lesson:

"In this lesson, you are going to practice preparing for and presenting one viewpoint in a debate, even if it's not something you personally believe. This will sharpen your skills at presenting a clear position and backing it up with evidence."

2. If needed, review the concept of debate, including the terms "pro" and "con."

3. Help students make a personal connection to this learning:

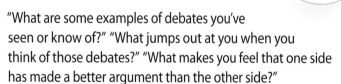

"What are some examples of debates you've seen or know of?" "What jumps out at you when you think of those debates?" "What makes you feel that one side has made a better argument than the other side?"

If students have a hard time naming examples, prompt them to think about anything currently happening such as debates about local issues, presidential debates, or court cases they might know about.

4. Have students talk with a partner; then invite a few volunteers to share with the group one thing they and their partner discussed.

5. Warm up with the Pros and Cons interactive learning structure (p. 63). Acknowledge that students might find this activity challenging because they might need to argue for something they don't personally believe. Remind them that doing this will help them understand both sides of the argument. Also let students know that this is just a warm-up; they'll be exploring these two sides more deeply in a few minutes.

Interactive Learning

6. Partner students and have them decide who is A and who is B. Designate A as "pro" and B as "con."

7. State the issue aloud to the group:

"Our school currently uses a ten-month school year calendar, with summer months off from school. Public schools in every state should now be required to use a twelve-month school year calendar, with vacation time scheduled every three months or so."

8. **Give everyone one minute to think.** Then, the "pro" person has one minute to state reasons for her side. Next, the "con" person has one minute to do the same. Both students then have thirty seconds to respond to the other person's statements, supporting their ideas with reasons.

9. Debrief the activity with the whole class, focusing on which were most compelling.

Body ✳ 60–70 Minutes

1. Let students know they're going to be assigned a "side" for the idea they used in the warm-up and will need to accurately represent it, just as they did in the opening activity. However, they'll now explore each position more deeply.

2. **Divide the class into four groups.** Two groups will be assigned the position that public schools in every state should be required to use a twelve-month school year calendar, with vacation time scheduled every three months or so. The other two groups will be assigned the position that schools should be allowed to continue using a ten-month school year calendar, with summer months off from school.

3. **Students will work in their groups to create an argument for their side of the issue.** They will first spend some time gathering information for their position by using websites, podcasts, news reports, books, and other materials.

Things Kids Love to Do

They can then choose to present their argument as a commercial or a news broadcast that lasts about five minutes or less. Students can create posters or other visuals to accompany their presentations.

Academic Choice

1. _____
2. _____
3. _____

4. Students will have about twenty to thirty minutes for gathering information and thirty minutes to create and then practice the presentations.

While they work, circulate to coach, answer questions, and provide feedback. Be sure to provide time frames for students so they know how much time they have left to plan and rehearse.

5. Each group gives their presentation to the class. The audience is encouraged to ask thoughtful questions and make respectful comments about each presentation. If needed, use Interactive Modeling to review how to make respectful comments and ask thoughtful questions.

Interactive Modeling

Closing ✴ 10–15 Minutes

1. Have students journal about both sides of the debate using a focus statement or question, such as "I used to think … and now I think …" or "How has your opinion on this issue changed?" Encourage them to cite examples from the presentations.

Open-Ended Questions

???

2. Students share their ideas with a partner.

FINAL THOUGHT: A PACE THAT WORKS

This three-part lesson structure sets a pace that makes sense for students—a brief opening, ample time to dig into the learning, and then a time to pause and reflect. Keeping this structure in mind as you plan will help you infuse lessons with elements that bring learning alive.

Giving Students Choices

Students in Ms. Gill's fourth grade classroom are getting ready to practice computation skills in preparation for an upcoming assessment test. She gives them four options for how to practice:

1. Use a website that has videos and quizzes.

2. Use Blackboard videos and practice sheets created by the teacher.

3. Create word problems—one problem for each type of computation.

4. Write about math in response to challenge questions, such as "How would you explain multiplication to a third grader?"

After reviewing the choices, Ms. Gill says, "We talk a lot about 'good-fit' books and you are all so thoughtful about choosing good-fit books that will help you become better readers. This is the same kind of choice. You'll be making a choice that will best help you practice computation."

She then uses a "think-aloud" strategy (see page 127) to demonstrate one way to think through this choice.

"I'm going to pretend I have a microphone in my head so you can hear my thoughts. 'I'd like to try writing about math but the Internet has been out at home and I haven't been able to get on Blackboard to do the practice sheets so I think I'll pick that option.' What did you notice about what I did?"

One student responds, "You thought about how you can do the practice sheets." Another says, "You wanted to practice but your Internet was out."

She gives students a moment to think about their "good-fit" choice.

Several students say that they want to use the website with videos and quizzes and a few choose the Blackboard videos and practice sheets. Habiba says that she usually chooses practice sheets so this time she's going to try a different method, creating word problems.

After the discussion, students record their choices on the sign-up chart and are soon hard at work. Ms. Gill circulates to coach and answer questions. She helps one student get started creating word problems: "First you write the number problem, then you go back and tell a story about that problem." As she talks the student's eyes light up. "Oh!" he exclaims. "Can I start with addition?" "Yes," Ms. Gill replies, "you can start anywhere you want to." He eagerly begins writing down ideas.

She pauses by another student's desk and watches for a moment as he works on a practice sheet. "What kind of numbers are you choosing to go on this side?" she asks. He shows her his work. "You're choosing friendlier numbers. That's a great strategy," she responds.

After working for twenty minutes, students gather for a brief reflection on their work. Ms. Gill asks, "How did your choice today help you with your learning?" Students talk with partners and then a few share thoughts with the whole class.

Andrew says that he worked through all the problems on his practice sheet. Habiba smiles and says she learned how to make word problems.

At the end, everyone does a private Fist to Five reflection (see page 133), assessing how comfortable they are with computation skills. Ms. Gill makes a mental note to check in later with a few students who didn't speak up during the reflection to see if they feel ready for the upcoming assessment test.

––––––––––––––

Ms. Gill's math review is an example of an Academic Choice lesson—a way of giving students a measure of teacher-guided control over what they learn or how they learn it (and sometimes both).

Academic Choice uses a three-part structure of planning, working, and reflecting that fits nicely into the three-part lesson structure you learned about in Chapter 5.

In the **planning** phase (opening), teachers present the choices and help students select an option that will help them meet their learning goals. During the **working** phase (body), teachers offer support as children follow through on the choice they made during planning. And during **reflecting** (closing), teachers offer prompting questions that help students think about how their work turned out, what they learned, and how their choices helped or hindered that learning.

This clear, three-part structure facilitates planning and implementing Academic Choice. In this chapter, we'll look more closely at how Academic Choice works and offer some practical strategies that will help you integrate it into your daily teaching.

Benefits of Academic Choice

* **Contributes to students' sense of autonomy.** We typically offer many kinds of choices during daily lessons. For example, we may invite students to choose which six of ten questions to answer, to decide whether to show their learning by making a poster or a video, to work with a partner or by themselves. These choices give students a degree of control over their daily life at school, which helps them engage more deeply with academic work.

Academic Choice strengthens and deepens this engagement. "You'll be making a choice that will best help you practice computation," Ms. Gill says in the opening vignette. With these words, she not only creates a space for autonomy but also gives children responsibility for their own learning. Navigating teacher-structured choices increases students' sense of pride in and ownership of their learning.

* **Helps to differentiate instruction.** Offering choices enables teachers to address a range of learning needs and aptitudes. With our guidance, students can choose to work at a level that feels just right—a level that

> **Benefits of Academic Choice:**
>
> ➤ Contributes to students' sense of autonomy
>
> ➤ Helps to differentiate instruction
>
> ➤ Can lead to increased achievement

challenges them enough to stretch their learning while still enabling them to feel successful.

Offering choices also gives students an opportunity to experience a range of ways to learn and practice content, which can keep things fresh and increase interest and motivation.

✳ **Can lead to increased achievement.** A University of Virginia study on the impact of *Responsive Classroom* implementation on academic achievement showed an association between use of the Academic Choice structure and improved performance in math and reading (Rimm-Kaufman et al., 2012). And a 2008 meta-analysis of 41 studies found a strong link between students' being given choices and their overall academic performance (Patall, Cooper, & Robinson, 2008). These findings support what teachers have long observed in their classrooms: When children feel in control of and connected to their learning tasks, they're more likely to do the work needed for success.

F A Q • By offering all these choices, don't I give up a lot of control?

Although we offer students choices and some control over what and how they learn, we never hand over all of that responsibility. We name the lesson objective, plan the lesson, and expect students to take part as they would with any lesson—they don't get to decide whether or not they practice math facts or do research or write a persuasive essay. They just get a measure of control over how they'll do that work.

We also decide what choices students will have based on our knowledge of students' strengths and needs; with our guidance and coaching, they choose among those options.

Getting Started

What kinds of lessons work with Academic Choice?

Academic Choice is a versatile practice that you can use in a wide range of lessons, from simple to complex:

* Practice basic skills, such as math facts or spelling sight words

* Practice fluency and decoding in reading

* Practice genres of writing

* Research and study a science, history, or social studies topic

* Look deeper into math concepts, such as geometry or fractions

* Show understanding or mastery of any curriculum standard

Throughout this chapter you'll see examples of Academic Choice lessons in action. In addition, several of the lesson plans in Chapter 5 incorporate choices of what or how to learn:

* In the kindergarten plan for retelling a story (p. 106), students choose how to show their retelling

* In the third/fourth grade lesson (p. 110), students choose which rock to describe

* In the sixth grade lesson (p. 113), students choose how to present their argument

---

F A Q • Can I build choice into a set curriculum?

Having a set curriculum with daily lessons plotted out needn't prevent you from offering choices. When Rosalea Fisher's school adopted new reading and spelling texts she initially felt constrained by the lesson plans, but soon realized that there were many ways to stick to the lessons and still offer choices.

For example, the curriculum called for reading and then responding to *Tony's Bread* by Tomie dePaola. Ms. Fisher offered four choices for responding to the story: create an advertisement for Tony's bread (drawing and writing); write a sequel; create an interview with Tony; act out a favorite part of the story. Students loved the lesson and created thoughtful responses—and met the curriculum's learning goals.

Academic Choice lesson: Fourth grade language arts

Lesson goal: Make a text-to-self connection to a fiction text. Create something to share that connection.

Choice: How to learn—students choose what medium to use to share their connection.

Planning: Ms. Kohler's fourth grade students have just finished reading the first chapter of *Island of the Blue Dolphins* by Scott O'Dell. She wants them to demonstrate understanding by making text-to-self connections. After a review of how to make text-to-self connections, she gives them a sentence stem to complete: "When I read _____ in chapter 6, it made me think about _____." She asks students to jot down ideas about how they might complete the sentence.

She then gives them three choices of how to demonstrate their connection: They can paint or draw a scene, make a cut-and-paste picture with captions, or write a story or poem. Students sign up for their choice on a chart, gather their needed materials, and go to the work space of their choice.

Working: They have twenty minutes to work as Ms. Kohler circulates to observe and coach. She notices that many students have chosen to make a cut-and-paste picture and a few are taking that a step further and making collages.

Ephraim, who usually writes, is experimenting with drawing a picture. "You're trying something new, Ephraim," she says. "You're stretching yourself."

"I just got this picture in my brain," he says. "I thought I could draw it better than write it."

Reflecting: At the end of the lesson, everyone meets in the circle space with their painting, picture, or piece of writing. Going around the circle, each person shows what they did and shares their completed sentence.

Ephraim goes first. He holds up his drawing of a house and a school building with a figure standing next to each and says, "When I read that the people on the island had two names, a public name and a private name, it made me think about how I have a nickname at home and a different nickname at school."

When to offer your first Academic Choice lessons

You can offer simple Academic Choice lessons early in the year, giving students "low stakes" choices—which of two picture books to look at or whether they'll use pencil and paper or a small whiteboard to practice their spelling. At the end of the lesson, help children reflect on the choice they made. What worked well? What might they do differently next time?

As children become more adept at making these simple selections, begin to offer choices that require more nuanced thinking. For example, students might choose what topic to focus on for a persuasive essay; whether to use a Venn diagram, essay, or table to compare and contrast their two favorite planets; or which book they'll review for classmates.

In early Academic Choice lessons, you'll also need to consider students' abilities to collaborate safely and successfully. Unless students have a lot of experience with collaborative learning from earlier grades and can work together productively, you might want students to work individually for your earliest Academic Choice lessons. As their collaborative skills grow, you can introduce lessons that enable them to work together.

The Three Phases of Academic Choice

Here's a closer look at the three phases of planning, working and reflecting.

Planning

The five- to fifteen-minute planning phase serves as the lesson opening. Students consider the choices offered and select the one that will help them meet the goals of the lesson and their own learning goals.

Here are the things you'll do as the planning phase unfolds.

Clearly state the goal or purpose

Engaged learning is purposeful and students benefit from hearing a simple statement of "why" at the beginning of a lesson. You might draw on curriculum standards when you think about a lesson's purpose, but in presenting the purpose to children, use student-friendly language and name how this work will benefit them as people—for example, by helping them become thoughtful, knowledgeable readers or helping them practice math skills that they'll use throughout second grade, and beyond. When students hear this "why," they begin to connect making a choice with reaching a goal.

Aim for a simple, clear statement that gives children a context for choosing: "Today we're beginning a unit on reading nonfiction texts. These are books that give information, rather than tell stories. To help us become thoughtful readers who can learn things we want to know from reading nonfiction, we're going to identify important elements of these kinds of books."

Offer choices that connect to the goal

Plan choices that clearly connect to the purpose of the lesson. For example, in the opening vignette all the choices Ms. Gill offered clearly connected to the goal of reviewing and practicing computation.

* **Offer choices that call on familiar skills.** To keep the focus on making a choice that will best meet goals, be sure to offer choices that students are familiar with. This is not a time to teach students how to use a Venn diagram or make a cut-and-paste picture—that teaching happens best in the context of other lessons and activities.

* **Limit the number of choices.** It's best to offer no more than four or five options. More than that could overwhelm students and make it hard to choose wisely.

* **Vary the number of choices as you go through the year.** Base the number on how well students are handling making a choice and what choices are needed to meet the learning goal for that particular lesson. For example:

  ➤ If the learning goal is to practice identifying fractions that are greater than, less than, or equivalent to other fractions and students are using a set of problems from a workbook, two choices—using fraction bars or drawing pictures—may be enough.

➤ On the other hand, if the learning goal is to demonstrate understanding of equivalent fractions by using a set of fractions, you may want to offer more options: write a story, use clay to create a display, or draw illustrations.

✳ **Pay attention to differentiating learning.** Offer choices that address all skill levels and interests in the class. For example, practicing math facts could include choices of manipulatives, such as dice, cards, spinners, coins, counters, or interlocking cubes; a worksheet; or math apps on a tablet.

Present the choices

How you present the choices has an impact on students' investment in the lesson and on their ability to make the selection that will best support their learning. As you tell students about the choices, use words that will prompt them to consider their needs and interests as learners. For example:

"Now that you've listed famous people in history that you would like to meet and get to know better, choose one to write about. Look over your list. Which one seems most interesting or important to you, one that you could write about for five minutes today?"

Examples of Choices to Offer

WHAT TO LEARN

➤ Which famous historical person to research

➤ Which of a list of math problems to solve

➤ Which of two or three teacher-stated positions on a controversial issue to argue for

HOW TO LEARN

➤ Practice vocabulary words by making flash cards, writing a paragraph using the words, or drawing a picture to represent the meaning of each word

➤ Take notes by underlining, writing in a notebook, or highlighting text

➤ Use manipulatives, dry erase boards, or tablets to work with math concepts or facts

➤ Share research results through writing, drawing a diagram, creating a song, or giving an oral report

---

F A Q • Is the planning phase a time for teachers to plan?

Teachers new to Academic Choice sometimes confuse this five- to fifteen-minute planning phase with their own planning of the lesson. As with any lesson, teacher planning takes place before you offer the Academic Choice lesson. The planning phase refers only to student planning.

Academic Choice lesson: First grade math

Lesson goal: Practice addition by creating and solving equations.

Choice: How to learn—students choose what tool to use (dice, number cards, or spinners).

Planning: First grade teacher Mr. Dupré wants students to practice addition by creating equations and then solving them.

He presents three choices of familiar tools to use—dice, number cards, or spinners—and reviews how students might use each one to create a simple equation. A quick discussion of why a student might select one tool over another helps children understand the purpose of the choices: to practice in a way that helps them do their best work. When they've made their decision, students place magnetic nametags under their choice on a whiteboard.

Working: Mr. Dupré then gives each child their chosen material and directs them to a table. There's excited and focused conversation at the tables as children create a range of equations. He pauses next to Matthew, who is throwing dice and using the results to create his equations. He's written down five equations so far, complete with correct solutions. "Five equations! Looks like you're on a roll, Matt," Mr. Dupré comments. "Math is fun!" Matt says. Mr. Dupre offers a challenge to Matthew. "When you are ready, try rolling the dice three times and then find the sum of all three numbers."

Reflecting: After ten minutes, Mr. Dupré rings a chime and releases the tables one by one to put their materials away and come to the meeting circle. When all children are seated in the circle, he says, "I saw everyone working hard to create and solve equations. Would someone who used dice share how the dice helped you practice addition?" Matt's hand shoots up. "Dice made it easy to do lots of different equations," he reports. "I made ten, and I solved them all!"

Give examples or model steps as needed

Although you will be offering familiar choices, you might want to show examples or model how to do something for choices that are complex or that have only recently been taught. For example:

* In a third grade class, students will have a choice of ways to practice telling time. One of the choices is using Judy clocks, a tool that students have only recently learned to use, so the teacher and a student model how to indicate time on the Judy clock and then write the time on a wipe-off board.

* In a fifth grade art class, students will have a choice of media they can use to express emotion. The teacher holds up a drawing as one example of how an artist uses color to express feelings.

"Think-Alouds"

A strategy to help students think about how or what to choose is a teacher "think-aloud." For example, if you are offering students choices for practicing vocabulary words, you might do a think-aloud like this:

"Let's pretend I'm making this choice. I'm going to talk out loud to show you my thinking. 'Hmm . . . the last couple of times we worked with vocabulary I decided to make flash cards. That's an easy choice for me but I also like to write stories and want to get better at writing, so I think I'll choose to write a paragraph using the vocabulary words.'"

Help students make thoughtful choices

Give students time to think about which option will best help them learn. To support them, you can:

* Ask a focusing question, such as "Why might someone make this choice?" or "Which choice might work well for you today?"

* Model how to make a choice from the list presented.

* Having students talk through their choice with a partner.

Through repeated opportunities to make choices and your support in evaluating the effectiveness of their choices, students learn invaluable lessons about how to think ahead and judge what will best support their learning.

Provide a way for children to show their choice

Here are three options that work well for a variety of Academic Choice lessons, from the simple to the complex.

✳ **Verbally name their choice.** For quick and simple Academic Choice lessons, students can think about and then name their choices as you call on them one at a time. Making quick notes about students' selections will help you plan future lessons (for example, you may discover that many students enjoy working with a particular material or format). Your notes will also help you assess students' choice-making skills: Do they tend to go with whatever their friends choose, or do they look for options that fit their learning needs? Do they choose similar options again and again, or do they take risks and stretch themselves by trying new things?

✳ **Sign their name on a choice board.** This method also works well for simple Academic Choice lessons. You display a chart of available choices and either record students' names on the chart as they name their choices or have students sign the chart themselves.

At times, you'll need to limit the number of children who sign up for a particular choice. For example, if one option is to do Internet research and only five computers have Internet access, put just five lines under that choice.

To keep the process efficient, plan how you'll invite students to sign up on the chart, and vary the order so the same children don't always make the first or last choice. For example, you could call on students in alphabetical or reverse alphabetical order, by birthdate, or by randomly picking names out of a box.

✳ **Use written planning sheets.** These can provide support for longer or more complex lessons. Planning sheets might have spaces for students to:

➤ Name their choice

➤ Note materials they'll need

➤ Outline a plan for how they'll do the work

Sample Student Planning Sheet
Grade 5, Research Project

Name: _____ Date: _____
Content area: _____
The topic I'll research is _____
The research sources I want to use are: _____
_____
_____
_____

Other materials I'll need are: _____
_____
_____
_____

My finished product to show what I've learned will be (choose one):
❑ Booklet
❑ Poster plus oral presentation
❑ PowerPoint plus oral presentation

My due dates are:
_____ Complete my research
_____ Turn in my draft for review
_____ Finish my booklet, poster, or PowerPoint

_____   _____
(Student)   (Teacher)

➤ Write or sketch what the finished product will look like (if applicable)

➤ Include a timeline with specific due dates for various parts or steps of a project (if applicable)

Student and teacher review the plan together and sign off on it.

Planning sheets help students organize their thinking and stay on track as they work. They also provide a starting point for discussion between teacher and student—as you review the plan, you might suggest refinements that will help a student be more successful.

Working

This phase (which corresponds to the body of the lesson) takes from fifteen or twenty minutes for a simpler lesson to up to several work periods for something like a research project. In the working phase, students bring their choices to life. They practice using a tool or material, experiment with and explore ideas, encounter and solve problems, and reset their course as needed.

F A Q • **Should I intervene when a child makes a less than optimal choice?**

Sometimes, even with your proactive support, a student will make a choice that you know is not the best one. Whether to intervene or not is a judgment call. If a choice is going to lead the child far astray from the learning goals or cause disruption for other learners, you'll most likely need to intervene. But making a less than optimal choice can provide a teachable moment. Did they choose something that was too easy, which might result in their being bored with the work? Or too difficult, which could lead to frustration? Having the child follow through on the choice and then reflect on it later can help the child make better choices in the future.

Here are ways you can support students during the working phase.

Pay attention to transitions

A smooth transition from planning to working helps establish a calm, focused atmosphere. Make sure children:

* Know how to move safely and quietly to the work space

* Are familiar with materials and can access them independently

* Have the skills needed to enact their choices

To prepare for productive work time, use Interactive Modeling to teach and review routines and use and care of materials (Appendix B). You can also use Guided Discovery to explore creative ways to use materials (see page 81).

When you see students following expectations, support them with reinforcing language (Appendix A): "You all got your art materials quickly and quietly. That helps everyone get down to work right away."

Observe

Following are some specific things to look for when observing students during Academic Choice lessons:

* ✴ Who makes thoughtful choices and who is swayed by peers' choices
* ✴ Who regularly follows through on plans and who repeatedly shifts course midstream
* ✴ Who sustains focus and who is easily distracted

These observations will guide your feedback and other interventions during the working phase of the lesson and beyond.

Give feedback

Positive feedback reassures students and helps them continue to work productively. For example, you could reinforce students' efforts by saying, "I see everyone is staying focused on their chosen task and doing the work they planned."

Facilitate and coach

Ask open-ended questions to guide students' work, offer direction or help to students who might need it, and give brief, focused instruction when needed and wanted. (For more about coaching, see page 101).

Help students manage time

Many students struggle with pacing their work so that they complete it in the time allotted. Here are simple things you can do to help:

* ✴ Be clear about the time frame and then give a warning halfway through the work period and another warning five minutes before the work period will end.
* ✴ Use a large timer or other time-keeping device that students can see from anywhere in the classroom.
* ✴ Pay attention to the kinds of materials children are using and give earlier cleanup time warnings to those using messier materials, such as watercolor paints or glue.

Reflecting

This five- to fifteen-minute phase closes the Academic Choice lesson. In this phase, students consider their work and the choices they made. They can do this individually, with a partner, in a small group, or as a whole class. Reflecting helps students assimilate and consolidate what they've learned, think about how their choices and actions influence the outcomes of their work, and get ideas for new directions in their future work. Thinking and talking about work can also provide a sense of closure that makes it easier for students to disengage from the task and move on to another topic or activity. Keep in mind that you might need several reflecting sessions if all students are presenting work.

What to reflect on

Reflection can focus on the following, either singly or in combination:

* The process of the work ("What would you do differently if you could do this work again?")

* The product ("What is a new fact you learned about _____ from your work?")

* The choice ("How did your choice help you . . . ?")

For example:

* At the end of a first grade PE class during which children chose one of three aerobic activities, the teacher does a quick reflection, asking students to hold up their fingers on a scale of zero to five to show how high their heart rate was raised during their activity.

* At the end of a writing choice lesson in a fifth grade classroom, the teacher does a longer reflection. She gathers the class in a circle and asks a few students to share how they revised their story's opening to capture the reader's attention. Classmates then ask the sharers questions about their work.

* During a multi-day research project, each day's work period might end with a brief reflection focused on process even though the working phase will continue for several days. A final reflection to encompass the entire lesson might be planned for the end of the project. At that time, students reflect on their overall process and present the results of their research.

Academic Choice lesson: Sixth grade social studies

Lesson goal: Research a key Civil War figure

Choice: What to learn—students choose from a list of five historical figures

Planning: Mrs. Siegel's sixth graders are just beginning a unit on the Civil War, in which they'll choose one of five people to research. She presents the five choices and then facilitates brainstorming of research questions, which include "What role did this person play in the Civil War?" "What motivated this person to take on this role?" "What other Civil War figures did this person interact with?"

Students sign up on a chart and Mrs. Siegel forms small working groups based on the choice of person.

Working: The small groups take one class period to research the class-generated questions, using books from the school library and websites bookmarked on the classroom tablets and computers. Mrs. Siegel observes, coaches, and troubleshoots when students get stuck in their research.

In the following class period, each group creates an illustrated poster to accompany an oral presentation about their person.

Reflecting: In the next two class periods, each group does their oral presentation for the class and takes questions and comments. After all groups have presented, Mrs. Siegel asks students to take a few minutes to write a journal entry: What is one thing you learned that surprised you, either in your own research or from classmates' presentations? What would you like to learn more about?

Help students connect their choices to their learning. Open-ended questions are a powerful way to help students make these connections. For example, you might ask: "How did your choice help or hinder your learning?" or "Do you think a different choice might have helped you learn more?" Such questions also tell students that learning to make good choices is a process. Through repeated reflections such as this, they'll hone their awareness of what makes a "good-fit" choice for their learning.

Sample Open-Ended Questions to Focus Reflection

- What is a new fact you learned about _____ from your work?

- How did your choice help you practice and learn more about _____?

- What is something you now know about _____ that you didn't before our work session?

- What is something else you want to learn about _____?

- How did your choice of content help you understand/learn the process?

- How has your learning changed your view/opinion on _____?

- What would you do differently if you could do this work again?

- What is one thing that surprised you about your work?

- What was one problem you had as you were working? How did you solve it?

Ways to reflect

These four ways of reflecting can be used alone or in combination.

Reflecting with a partner: Allows students to articulate thoughts and get feedback from a classmate. Supports sharing of ideas.

Reflecting with a small group: Allows sharing of ideas and learning from each other.

Four ways to reflect

Reflecting with the whole group: Allows sharing of ideas and learning from each other.

Silent reflection: For individual, sometimes private, reflection on process or learning.

Silent reflection.

Think to Yourself. You pose a focus question, such as "What's one new thing you learned from your work today?" and students have a minute or two to silently think of their answer to the question.

Thumb Gauge. This is a quick reflection. To answer a focus question such as "Do you think your choice helped you with your work today?" or "How well did you follow our class rules as you worked today?" students respond with thumbs-up ("yes" or "very well"), thumbs-sideways ("sort of" or "not sure"), or thumbs-down ("no" or "not very well"). Student responses can be public, with thumbs visible to all, or private, with thumbs held close to the body.

Fist to Five. This is another quick reflection similar to Thumb Gauge. Students respond to a focus question, such as "How well do you think you were able to work independently today?" or "How did you like the work you did today?" by holding up zero to five fingers. Zero (a fist) means "not at all." Five means "very well." As with Thumb Gauge, this can also be done privately with hands held close to the body.

Journaling. Students respond in writing to your focus question. Their writing can be brief (a sentence) or more complex (a paragraph or a letter to themselves). Young students can create a sketch or drawing as a response to a reflection question.

Agree, Disagree. Divide the classroom in half with an imaginary line, or designate two separate places in the room that students can move to. Designate one side or space for students who agree and the other for students who disagree. Then make a statement about the Academic Choice lesson students have just completed, for example, "I learned something new today from the work I did" or "I wish I had more time today to work." Students then move to the designated area that represents their response. You can continue the process with several more questions as time allows.

Reflecting with a partner.

Partner Chat. Partners take turns responding to your focus question. Depending on students' needs and abilities, you can assign partners or let students choose partners.

Interactive Learning Structures. Try one of the partner-based structures described in Chapter 3. Specifically, take a look at Inside-Outside Circles (p. 55), Mix and Mingle to Music (p. 58), and Swap Meet (p. 68).

Reflecting with a small group.

Around-the-Circle. Students take turns saying one thing in response to a focus question. If students were in small groups during the working phase, they might stay in those groups for the reflecting phase or you might form new groups specifically for reflecting.

Two-Four-Eight. Students pair up and each responds to a focus question. Then pairs join to form groups of four, and students share their answers from the previous pairing or respond to a new question. Foursomes then join to form groups of eight, and responses are shared one more time. If needed, provide a structure to ensure that all voices are heard (for example, students go around clockwise with each person saying one thing).

Interactive Learning Structures. You could also use a structure such as Maître d' (p. 57) or Four Corners (p. 53).

Reflecting with the whole group.

Around-the-Circle Sharing. Gathered in one large circle, students take turns briefly responding to your focus question. Before using this structure, model giving a focused, brief response. You can give students extra support by providing a sentence stem ("I did _____ because _____").

Simultaneous Display. Students sit in a circle and all those who wish to share their work hold it up or place it on the floor in front of them. Provide a focus, such as looking for new ideas, to guide the group in purposeful observation. This structure enables students to have their work seen and to gather ideas for future work from what classmates have done.

Individual Presentations of Work. Everyone gathers in a circle and individual students present their work—or work in progress—to the whole class in what is sometimes called a representing meeting.

Provide a focus to help structure the presentations, for example, "Tell us one thing that surprised you about _____."

These meetings might be as short as ten minutes, with everyone sharing very briefly or, for longer Academic Choice projects, they might extend over several sessions with three to five students sharing at each session.

For this sharing of work to be successful, it's important to teach presenters how to speak clearly and briefly in response to a focus question, and audience members need to learn how to listen closely and formulate useful and respectful questions and comments.

Interactive Learning Structures. You might also want to look at structures such as Museum Walk (p. 59) and Snowball (p. 67).

Introduce reflection structures carefully

As with interactive learning structures and other activities we've presented, careful introduction of the reflecting structure will help ensure student success. Think about the skills involved and use Interactive Modeling to teach new skills. For many of the reflecting structures, students will need to be comfortable with sharing one key idea, speaking loudly and clearly, listening respectfully, waiting their turn to speak, asking clarifying questions, and making supportive comments.

Help Children Succeed With Academic Choice

Academic Choice Is Built On		
Sense of safety and community	Independent work skills	Collaborative work skills

You begin laying the foundation for Academic Choice in the first days of school. You get to know students and help them get to know each other, and establish classroom rules that will enable everyone to work and play safely together. You also begin teaching students how to use and care for classroom materials, collaborate with each other, and do various academic activities, such as careful observation.

In short, you're building a sense of safety and community, students' independent work skills, and their collaborative work skills. This teaching is a must if students are to succeed in school, and this is the very same teaching that enables them to benefit from Academic Choice lessons.

Below are some key strategies to help strengthen classroom community and boost students' ability to work both independently and cooperatively.

Cultivate kindness, respect, and confidence

To get the most out of Academic Choice lessons, students need a safe, calm learning community in which their interactions with you and with each other are governed by kindness and respect. They need to feel comfortable and confident taking learning risks, making mistakes, working with classmates, and sharing information, ideas, and reflections with the whole group.

Building community is something that happens throughout the year. Each time you model a routine, reinforce students' efforts to meet expectations, group students thoughtfully, and teach them ways to work together, you're cultivating fertile ground for effective Academic Choice.

Teach use and care of materials

To succeed with the variety of options you'll offer through Academic Choice lessons, students must know how to access, use, and care for art materials, writing center supplies, math manipulatives, and science and technology equipment. Interactive Modeling and Guided Discovery are two strategies you can use for teaching children how to handle classroom materials.

✳ **Use Interactive Modeling (Appendix B) when you want students to use a material in a particular way.** For example, in the sixth grade example on page 132, students might want to use school-approved websites to research the topic, so you could do a couple of Interactive Modeling lessons to teach them how to use the search features on those sites.

✳ **Use Guided Discovery (Chapter 4) to explore a range of ideas for using materials.** For example, in the fourth grade example on page 122, students might have previously explored various ways to use art materials that they can draw on to create their representation of a text-to-self connection; in the first grade example on page 126, students might have had a Guided Discovery lesson exploring ways to use dice or spinners to support their learning.

	Interactive Modeling	Guided Discovery
Examples of materials	Use when you want students to learn one right way to use a material: Scissors Stapler Eraser Paintbrush Tablet or computer Camera	Use when you want students to explore multiple, creative uses of a material: Pencils Colored pencils Markers Graphic design software Pattern blocks Dictionary Modeling clay
Purposes	Teach clear expectations for safe use and care	Teach clear expectations AND build a repertoire of creative ideas

Model academic activities

Interactive Modeling is also a great strategy for teaching the academic activities students might do independently (that is, without your direct supervision) during an Academic Choice lesson. For example, you might model how to:

* Give peer feedback

* Create and add ideas to a Venn diagram

* Read with a partner

* Make observations

* Listen to a podcast or other recording

* Conduct an interview

* Participate in a class discussion

Teach communication and collaboration skills

Your Academic Choice lessons will likely offer students many formal and informal opportunities to talk and share with classmates. During the planning phase, they might talk with a partner about how they're deciding what to choose; during the reflecting phase, they might share thoughts with partners or small groups on how their choice worked out. And in many Academic Choice lessons, you'll want students in pairs or groups for the working phase.

Your efforts to build a safe learning community will go a long way toward making these collaborations productive, but you will also want to teach specific collaborative skills. See Chapter 2 to learn how to teach the skills needed for collaborative work and conversation and Chapter 3 for information about structures that support collaborative learning.

Teach routines for independent work

Academic Choice lessons often give students opportunities to work without your ongoing supervision, while you circulate and offer support as needed. To succeed with independent work, students need to learn how to:

* Stay focused on a task

* Get help if you're busy with other students

* Respond if someone's bothering them

* Calm themselves if they feel frustrated

Interactive Modeling (Appendix B) is a great way to teach students routines that will help them be independent learners. For example, you could use Interactive Modeling to teach students a signal they can use to let you know they need help when you're busy with other students.

Role-playing (see page 38) is a good strategy for helping students think through options for tricky situations such as responding to a classmate who is interrupting their work time or calming themselves when they feel frustrated.

Reteach skills as needed

As your learning community grows stronger and students' skills develop, they'll increasingly benefit from their Academic Choice lessons. But if you see students struggling with Academic Choice as the year goes on, you may find that you need to reteach one or more of the independent or collaborative work skills. Abbreviated Interactive Modeling (see Appendix B, page 175) is a great way to reteach skills.

Sample Academic Choice Lesson Plans

The following six sample Academic Choice lesson plans will give you an idea of the range of lessons that you can structure by letting children choose what or how to learn (or both). The Academic Choice Planning Guide template in Appendix C will help you structure your own Academic Choice lessons.

Math ✳ Addition

Goal: Practice the skill of addition.

What: Choice	**How:** Choice
Solve a set of addition problems. Offer 2–4 sets of addition problems for students to choose from. Each set should represent an ability level that matches the various ability levels of the students.	• Unifix cubes • Number line • Hundreds chart

Plan: Ask for or suggest reasons why a first grader might pick each of the three "How" choices. For example, some students might choose the number line to see the sequence of all the numbers involved in an addition problem; other students might want to work with Unifix cubes because they can build the answer using one-to-one correspondence. Students think about their own learning needs, then sign up for a choice and pick the set of problems they want to solve.

Work: Students use their choice of tools to solve math problems as you visit with students to observe, coach, and ask questions.

Reflect: Ask the whole group: "How did your tool help you solve the math problems? Is anyone interested in trying another tool next time? Why?"

Language Arts ✳ Opinion Piece

Goal: Practice writing an opinion piece.

What: Choice	**How:** No choice
Yes or no: Should we have more recess breaks during the school day?	Write an opinion piece with an introduction of the topic, reasons to support the opinion, linking words, and a conclusion.

Plan: To help students decide which opinion to support, ask, "What are some reasons for having more recess? What are some reasons why we shouldn't?" Students briefly consider their own thoughts about the appropriate amount of recess and then indicate which opinion they will write about.

Work: Students write independently as you circulate, providing feedback and asking questions.

To prepare for reflection, form partnerships among students.

Reflect: Students share their opinion and supporting details with a partner.

In whole-class discussion, students name convincing opinions they heard. Ask questions such as "What made them convincing?" "Did anyone change their opinion after hearing from someone else?"

Science ✳ Insects

Goal: Learn about insects.

What: Choice	**How:** Choice
Variety of materials for research, including print materials at various reading levels, online resources, videos, etc.	Students can work with a partner or individually to share what they've learned by: • Writing an essay • Making labeled drawings • Writing a song • Creating a graphic organizer

Plan: Suggest why students might select each of the four methods for sharing what they've learned. For example, students might choose to write a song if they learn best through music and movement. Drawing might be a good option for students who are visual learners. Students then sign up for the method they will use to share their knowledge and for resources if some are limited (such as technology). Assign partners for students who want to work with someone.

Work: Students gather facts and create a product to show what they've learned. You circulate, providing assistance, encouragement, and feedback and asking questions about the work.

Reflect: Students share what they have learned about insects with the class by responding to focus questions: "What is something new you discovered about insects?" "Did you discover something that surprised you?"

Social Studies ✳ Early Settlements

Goal: Compare and contrast early settlements.

What: Choice	**How:** Choice
All students will compare and contrast the same two settlements (for example: Jamestown and Plymouth). They can choose among a large variety of materials for gathering information, such as print materials at various reading levels, online resources, maps, videos, etc.	You will assign partners, but partnerships can choose to record information in one of three ways: • Venn diagram • Written outline • Timelines

Plan: Give suggestions to help partnerships make their choices. For example, partners who enjoy discovering how two events are interrelated might want to create timelines. Others might choose to create a written outline because this provides some scope for individual work. Partners could divide up the research and writing, and then come together later to combine ideas into one document.

Partnerships sign up. Before releasing students to begin work, ask questions to help them plan: "What information will you need to gather first?" "Where will you find this information?" "How will you take notes?"

Work: Partnerships gather materials and find a spot to begin work. You circulate to observe, coach, provide feedback, and ask questions to stretch and extend learning.

Reflect: Have each pair join with another—ideally one that made a different "How" choice—and then the pairs in each foursome take turns sharing a summary of their work.

In a whole-group discussion, share key findings about similarities and differences. Also ask: "Which settlement seemed most successful? Why?" "Which seemed to struggle? Why?"

Guidance or Counseling

Goal: Learn and practice strategies for calming down.

What: Choice	**How:** No choice
• Take deep breaths • Count • Clench and unclench hands • Close eyes and think of a special place	• Sit in a chair and practice your choice

Plan: Briefly model each choice. Prompt students to think about how they might decide which method to use. For example, a student might choose counting because that seems like something that might help them and they've never tried it before; another might want to do deep breathing because that's a familiar strategy that they use at home.

Work: Once students have chosen a method to try, give them a scenario in which a student is likely to become upset or angry. Students then practice their chosen self-calming method.

Reflect: Have students share how their choice helped them calm down. "How did your method help calm you?" "How could it help you in other situations where you might become angry or upset?" "Is there another strategy you want to try next time?"

144   The Joyful Classroom

Physical Education

Goal: Practice basketball skills.

What: Choice	**How:** No choice
Which basketball skill to work on: • Dribbling • Passing (work with a partner) • Shooting	Practice skill in designated area.

Plan: Give examples of why students might choose one skill over another to practice. For example, a student might choose shooting because it's an area they want to improve in; another might want to practice passing because they want to work with a partner.

Students sign up; you assign partners for those who want to practice passing. Students get a ball and move to the designated space for practicing their choice.

Work: As students are working, circulate to support, demonstrate, encourage, and coach.

Reflect: Have students share how their choice helped them to practice. What improvements did they make? What did they learn as they were practicing?

FINAL THOUGHT: THE GIFT OF CHOICE

When we offer students choices we give them a valuable gift. The skills they learn—how to make wise choices, how to enact those choices and learn from them, how to adjust and adapt when needed—will serve them well throughout school and help them become lifelong learners.

WORKS CITED

Patall, E. A., Cooper, H., & Robinson, J. C. (2008, March). The Effects of Choice on Intrinsic Motivation and Related Outcomes: A Meta-Analysis of Research Findings. *Psychological Bulletin* 134(2), 270–300.

Rimm-Kaufman, S. E., Larsen, R., Curby, T., Baroody, A., Merritt, E., Abry, T., Ko, M., & Thomas, J. (2012, September). *Efficacy of the Responsive Classroom Approach: Results From a Three Year, Longitudinal Randomized Controlled Trial.* Paper presented at the meeting of the Society for Research in Educational Effectiveness, Washington, DC.

Teaching Students to Self-Assess

In Ms. Johnson's fifth grade class, students are learning about persuasive writing. They've read and discussed persuasive essays, identified key elements of the genre, engaged in debates, and each chosen a topic. Now students are ready to write drafts of their essays.

Ms. Johnson begins by naming the lesson goal: To write an essay that includes the fundamental elements of persuasion. She posts criteria for good work on the whiteboard and gives each student a checklist of grade-appropriate elements of persuasive writing, for example, "You have an introduction that clearly states your position" and "You give at least three reasons or examples that support your position."

She then asks students to take a moment and think of their personal goal for this essay and to record that goal in their writing journal.

Soon, students are busy writing their essays, referring to the checklist often as they work. Ms. Johnson circulates, observing and checking in with students. She stops by Caleb's desk. He has chosen the topic "Spending more time at recess each day would benefit students." Ms. Johnson asks if there's something in his draft he'd like her to pay attention to and he tells her about his personal goal—to work on supporting his ideas with evidence. With that in mind, she reviews his draft.

"Tell me more about your third reason for having a longer recess," she asks him.

"I was thinking that recess could be longer because then we'd have time to play more than one game," Caleb says.

Ms. Johnson pauses for a moment and then asks, "How does this support your main point? How might having time to play more than one game be useful or helpful for kids?" Caleb nods his understanding and returns to his writing.

At the end of the writing period, Ms. Johnson projects onto the board a persuasive writing rubric. She asks students to compare their draft to the criteria on the rubric. After they've had time to reflect, Ms. Johnson asks, "What is one piece of your draft that you think meets a level three or four? What is one thing you'd like to work on in revision? Take a minute and think and then make a note in your journal."

Caleb notes that he added ideas to his third reason and it now is at a level four. For a next step, he wants to revise his concluding paragraph.

––––––––––––––––––––

In school, the word "assessment" is often linked to testing, grading, and ranking. But, as shown in this vignette, assessment can also mean simply taking a look at where one is in relation to a goal, what one is doing well, and what course corrections might be appropriate—and that's a skill we can use throughout our lives. For example, I recently started playing the piano for the first time since adolescence. My goal was to accompany friends in informal music-making. I bought some books and started making my way through lessons, trying to assess how much I remembered and what I'd need to learn.

I quickly knew I'd need a teacher. Fortunately, I found one who encouraged my pausing regularly to reflect on my progress. "What feels too easy?" she'd ask. "What is too difficult?" "In what ways do you feel that you are improving?" My answers helped us both understand what information and practice I still needed so that I could reach my learning goal. I was engaging in a process of self-assessment.

In this chapter, we offer self-assessment tools and strategies students can use as aids in meeting their learning goals. This goal-related self-assessment is *formative*; that is, it provides information to help students make adjustments throughout the process of *forming* their skills and understanding. This kind of self-assessment can be as simple as having students consult a checklist of expectations as they work on a project or reflect to themselves on what they learned from an activity. Or students might complete a written self-evaluation of a finished product. Whether simple or more complex, self-assessment helps students monitor and evaluate their own work and identify ways to improve their learning.

How Does Self-Assessment Benefit Student Learning?

When built into daily schoolwork, goal-focused self-assessment fosters academic achievement by helping students:

* **Develop valuable lifelong skills,** including the ability to think critically about their own work; know themselves and their learning styles; reflect on their individual strengths and challenges; and measure their progress toward goals.

* **Become autonomous learners** who take responsibility for their learning and become actively engaged in the academic life of the classroom.

* **Develop a growth mindset.** Self-assessment helps students develop what social psychologist Carol Dweck calls a growth mindset—the belief that basic qualities (such as the ability to learn new things) are not fixed, but can be cultivated through personal effort and persistence (Dweck, 2010). Students with a growth mindset, Dweck says, want to improve; they seek out learning, stretch themselves, and develop more effective learning strategies.

> **Benefits of Student Self-Assessment**
>
> ➤ Develops lifelong skills
>
> ➤ Helps students become autonomous learners
>
> ➤ Develops a growth mindset
>
> ➤ Builds resilience

* **Build resilience.** Self-assessment helps students understand their learning process and consider how to take on learning challenges. Faced with a difficult task, they think about strategies they've used in the past to grapple with new material, increase concentration, or keep going when things got hard. They then decide how to apply those strategies to their current challenge. As a result, they become stronger, more resilient learners.

Ultimately, teaching self-assessment helps us give children the true gift of education: the recognition that they can grow and change and an innate desire to do so.

Foster a Growth Mindset

A growth mindset and the habit of self-assessment are reciprocal. As one grows, so does the other: Regular use of self-assessment tools promotes a growth mindset, and a growth mindset promotes the productive use of self-assessment tools.

To get this cycle going, it's important to continually nurture a classroom environment in which all children believe they can be successful learners, no matter what their grades have been in the past or how they score on various standardized tests. In other words, you want to keep the classroom tone tilted toward growth.

Your teacher language (Appendix A) is one important tool for setting this tone. In addition, you can use stories and analogies, which make abstract information concrete and accessible for young learners.

F A Q • When is the best time to have students self-assess?

Goal-related self-assessment is most effective if students assess work in progress so they can make changes as they go along. Think of the drafting and editing process you teach students in writing workshop. This process of pausing, checking in, and revising can apply to any other classroom work.

I often stopped students during working periods to have them quickly check in with the criteria for good work I'd posted on the board or to give themselves a thumbs-up, thumbs-down, or thumbs-in-the-middle for how they were doing with partner work or small-group collaboration. They could then go back to work with a fresh perspective or new goal for improvement.

Teacher language sets the tone

Suppose that, like Ms. Johnson in the opening vignette, you're getting students started on drafting their persuasive essays. You might say, "Wow, you all are learning so much about how to craft a good argument. As I listened to your debates I heard clear statements of a point of view and facts and evidence to support your position. You are ready to take the next step and turn your strong thinking into persuasive essays."

With words like these, you reinforce students' efforts and inspire them with a clear message: Learning is a process and everyone can learn and grow.

From day one, the words you use to introduce lessons and to support children as they work help them understand what is valued in the classroom community: taking on challenging tasks, taking risks, sticking with something even if it's hard, and trying a variety of strategies to solve a problem. Two kinds of teacher language are particularly effective in conveying this message:

* **Envisioning language lets students know you believe they're ready for the adventure of learning and entices them to come along.**

> "You've all been working so hard; I know you're ready for this reading challenge and all the fascinating new things you'll be able to learn by reading at this level."

> "This math work is like climbing a mountain—it can be tough to get started, but you'll quickly get warmed up. And if you keep climbing, you'll get to the top; the view from up there is amazing!"

Envisioning statements like these convey to students that you believe in them and in their ability to tackle the work.

* **Reinforcing language encourages children as they learn.**

> "I see that you've been trying a variety of strategies to solve this problem. You're not giving up on this!"

> "You searched for a long time to find the answer to your question about lightning. Now you can teach us what you've learned."

Reinforcing statements like these recognize students for their hard work, for the learning process they're engaged in, and for their successes along the way.

Keep the focus on process

For envisioning and reinforcing language to be most effective, it's important to focus on process—on what strong learners do—rather than on fixed attributes such as intelligence or aptitude.

* **In envisioning statements,** avoid using words such as "gifted" or "talented." Instead, focus on traits that are malleable and action-oriented, traits that all students can aspire to develop in themselves, by using words such as "hard-working" or "motivated."

* **When reinforcing students' efforts,** instead of praising their intelligence, focus on and encourage positive steps they've taken. If a student finishes a piece of work quickly and with good results, you might be tempted to say, "You are so smart! You got that right away!" But such words convey that what you value most is their being "smart."

To cultivate a growth mindset, put the focus on their process, saying, "You finished so quickly. How did you do that?"

This helps a student reflect on the effort they put into the work and the efficient strategies they used and lets them know that success is within their control.

Use stories to illustrate the power of hard work

You can utilize children's love of stories to help them develop a growth mindset and send an important message about the power of hard work and the possibility of growth and change. Following are two ways to use stories:

* **Share biographies** of people who have become successful through hard work to help inspire and encourage students. In my fourth grade classroom, picture books such as *Thank You, Mr. Falker* by Patricia Polacco and *Wilma Unlimited* by Kathleen Krull, and chapter books such as *Wonder* by R. J. Palacio, *Matilda* by Roald Dahl, and the Harry Potter series by J. K. Rowling sparked wonderful discussions about reaching success through perseverance and grit.

* **Share personal stories** of learning from mistakes or of overcoming obstacles, sticking with a challenge, and not giving up. I had a colleague who ran the Boston Marathon every year, and she often shared with her students the challenges of running in the winter and sticking with her training plan

despite cold, dark, snowy mornings. She described how this hard work led to the joys of finishing long runs with friends and finally crossing the finish line on race day.

Teach how brains can grow and change

Second grade teacher Hannah Whitaker is wrapping up a newly introduced math activity called Beat the Calculator. "I could almost see your brains growing as you tried out math strategies," she says, pointing to the strategies listed on a chart. "If you keep at it, these strategies will build your brain muscle and help all of you become stronger mathematicians, able to solve more and more interesting problems."

Students need to know that with effort they can develop and strengthen their brains, and analogies are a great way to get this message across. Like Ms. Whitaker, you might invite students to visualize their brain as a muscle that needs to exercise and practice, just like the muscles in their legs or arms.

In the book *Your Fantastic Elastic Brain*, author JoAnn Deak uses the analogy of an elastic band. She explains that students can stretch their elastic brains when they make mistakes and take risks, and that "you really can train your brain to be fit and strong and to keep stretching and growing throughout your whole life!" (Deak, 2010, p. 25).

Self-Assessment and Goal-Setting Go Hand in Hand

Self-assessment is tied to goal-setting, which begins with learners realistically assessing where they are and then deciding on a meaningful and realistic goal they want to reach.

Generating ideas and goals

Reflecting on experiences

Actively exploring, experimenting, problem-solving

As they work toward that goal, their periodic assessments can help them know if they're on the right track or if they need to adjust course or refine their goal. This process reflects the natural learning cycle you learned about in the introduction to this book.

Begin the year with a message of goals and growth

Many teachers who use the *Responsive Classroom* approach begin the year by asking students to articulate hopes and dreams (or broad goals) for the year's learning. Through a process of guided reflections, students name hopes and dreams such as "I hope to get better at multiplication" or "I want to do more science experiments."

Whether or not you lead children through the full process of developing hopes and dreams, taking the time to reflect with them on broad learning goals opens the year with a message of possibility and growth. It also sets a tone that helps them feel invested in working to achieve their specific learning goals throughout the year.

Encourage goal-setting throughout the year

Although you will set lesson-by-lesson goals, often in accordance with district or state standards, students can have a voice in setting their own learning goals throughout the year. In your opening to a lesson, encourage students to consider what they want to practice or learn and to set a personal goal for each lesson.

For example, in the opening vignette, Ms. Johnson named a lesson goal—"To write an essay that includes the fundamental elements of persuasion"—and then asked students to set personal goals related to that larger goal.

Effective Learning Goals Are:

➤ **Specific.** "I'd like to learn how to convert decimals to fractions" lays out a much clearer path for a student than the more general "I'd like to improve my math skills."

➤ **Attainable.** Goals need to be age-appropriate and within reach for the student in the specified time frame. A third grader who wants to be an astronomer might choose as a school-year goal learning the names of all the planets along with their sizes, the names of their moons, and how far they are from the sun.

➤ **Relevant.** Goals need to be personally significant and important to a student's learning. If a student wants to play piano because her older brother plays, you might guide her to revise her goal to "I want to explore several instruments and choose the one I most enjoy playing."

➤ **Well-defined.** Asking, "How will you know you've achieved your goal?" will help students visualize meeting the goal. The question also helps them assess whether the goal is right for them: If they struggle to answer the question, they probably need to go back and refine the goal to make it more specific, attainable, or relevant.

In a math class, the lesson goal might be to practice multiplication facts. One student might have a personal goal of memorizing the answers to a certain set of facts (multiplying by 6 and by 7); another student might want to focus on increasing speed when using multiplication. Throughout the lesson, the self-assessment opportunities you structure can help students answer the question, "Is the work I'm doing helping me reach my learning goal?"

Self-Assessment Tools

Checklists, rubrics, and structures for reflection are all tools that can help students with self-assessment.

Checklists tell students what to include in their work

A checklist spells out what needs to be included in a piece of work. You might list, for example, the key elements of a fictional story, a plan for a science experiment, or the components of a commercial jingle.

Students drafting persuasive essays, as in the opening vignette, might consult a checklist to make sure they're including key elements of this type of writing:

* An introduction that clearly states their position

* At least three reasons or examples that support the position

* Each reason developed with details and evidence

* A conclusion that summarizes their argument

As students work on assignments, checklists serve as useful reminders of specific expectations and can help students stay focused and on task when working independently. Students can only be reminded of what they already know, so be sure your checklists contain items that you've already introduced to them. See two examples of checklists on the next page.

Persuasive Essay Checklist

Name: _____

My topic: _____

❏ I clearly state my position in the introduction.

❏ I give at least three reasons to support my position.

❏ I support each reason with details and evidence.

❏ I stay focused on the topic.

❏ My conclusion summarizes my argument.

Other things I want to make sure I do:

❏ _____

❏ _____

❏ _____

Notes: _____

_____

_____

_____

_____

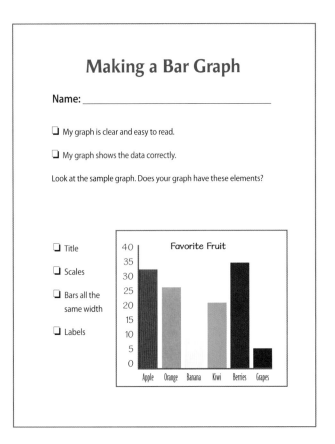

Making a Bar Graph

Name: _____

❏ My graph is clear and easy to read.

❏ My graph shows the data correctly.

Look at the sample graph. Does your graph have these elements?

❏ Title

❏ Scales

❏ Bars all the same width

❏ Labels

Rubrics help students assess how well they've met expectations

A rubric lists the criteria for good work. Rubrics might list levels of performance: for example, Ms. Johnson's rubric for the persuasive essay lesson might list the checklist elements and describe, for each one, what that element would look like in a piece of writing that was either advanced (level 4), proficient (level 3), approaching (level 2), or beginning (level 1). Rubrics might also state just the expectations for proficient work—level 3—with space for teachers to note ways in which a student's work falls short of or surpasses this standard. (See page 161 for examples.)

Whether you choose a multi-point or single-point format, your rubrics should provide students with important guidelines without constraining creativity. Criteria on a rubric should allow students the latitude to make choices in their learning and bring their own voice into their work.

Who creates the rubrics?

You might take sole responsibility for creating rubrics or you might involve students in the creation process. When students help create rubrics, they increase their understanding of lesson goals and expectations and are more invested in the lesson and in performing at a high standard.

Here are two tips for how to bring students' voices into creating rubrics:

* **Ask general questions about the work:** "How will we know it's 'good' work?" "What should we see if your ideas are working?" "What will make the assignment a success?"

* **Ask questions that help students access prior knowledge:** "What have we learned about the elements of nonfiction texts?" The resulting list can be incorporated into both a checklist and a rubric.

Introducing rubrics

Careful introduction helps students use rubrics effectively. Consider this example from a second grade classroom:

> Mr. Lin takes care from day one to create an atmosphere that supports a growth mindset. And it's in that spirit that he introduces use of rubrics during a unit on scientific observation and note-taking. He lets students know that they're going to begin working with rubrics to help them assess their own progress toward important goals.
>
> He says, "You might think it's only the teacher's job to use a rubric to look at student work. But this year, it will also be your job to look at your own work and to think about how well you are meeting the goals of doing strong scientific observation and note-taking. You'll also use our rubric to figure out what else you need to do to meet those goals."
>
> Mr. Lin begins by brainstorming with students the essential characteristics of scientific observation and note-taking. As students call out ideas he lists them on the interactive whiteboard: "You put down a lot of facts." "It's just what you see." "It's just about the thing you're looking at." He quickly uses this list to create a basic single-point rubric on the board, noting proficient performance expectations for observation and for note-taking.

He then says to the class, "Let's put these ideas to work." He gives students a page from a student's observation journal from a previous year to practice using the rubric. Students work together in pairs to discover how the notes match the expectations on the rubric. Mr. Lin again takes ideas from students, asking them for evidence to support their claims.

Once students have shared a range of ideas, Mr. Lin tells them that the student who wrote the journal used feedback from a rubric to set a new goal of adding more detail to his notes—more facts describing what he saw. He finishes the discussion by asking students to chat with their elbow partner about one item on the rubric they want to pay attention to in their upcoming work.

Use rubrics to support a growth mindset

To keep the process of using rubrics focused on growth, present them as tools that will help students learn and move forward. Then take time to help students understand how to use each rubric. You could present a sample rubric, as Mr. Lin did, and have students analyze a sample of their own work.

You could also have students look at a variety of sample pieces and use a rubric to assess the work. When students have a chance to analyze examples with varying levels of quality, they can understand what "proficient" work looks like and get a concrete idea of what they can do to stretch themselves to achieve that level of work.

Reflection helps students make sense of both content and process

To be effective with self-assessment, students need to develop their ability to think critically about the work they're doing. To help students learn and practice these critical thinking skills, you can build in time for reflection throughout their work block as well as during the closing segment of lessons. You can also use reflection along with checklists and rubrics. In the opening vignette, Ms. Johnson asks students to compare their drafts to the rubric and then reflect: "What is one piece of your draft that you think meets a level three or four? What is one thing you'd like to work on in revision?"

Persuasive Essay Rubric

Name: _____ Essay topic: _____

	4 - Advanced	3 - Proficient	2 - Approaching	1 - Beginning
Focus/topic/opening	Strongly and clearly states a personal opinion. Introduces the main points of the opinion/argument.	Clearly names the personal opinion. Makes some reference to the main points of the opinion/argument.	Personal opinion is not clearly stated. Makes little or no reference to the main points of the opinion/argument.	Personal opinion is not easily understood. Makes no reference to the main points of the opinion/argument.
Support for position	Includes three or more reasons for the opinion and each reason is supported by evidence (facts, statistics, examples). The writer addresses potential reader concerns, biases, or arguments and has provided at least one counter-argument.	Includes three or more reasons for the opinion and each reason is supported by evidence (facts, statistics, examples).	Includes two reasons for the opinion and provides minimal evidence for each reason (facts, statistics, examples).	Includes one reason for the opinion but provides little evidence to support the reason.
Transitions	Uses a variety of transitions that clearly show how ideas are connected.	Transitions show how ideas are connected. Uses some variety in transitions.	Some transitions are used; connections between ideas are not clear.	Transitions are unclear or not present.
Closing paragraph	The conclusion leaves the reader clearly understanding the writer's opinion. Author clearly summarizes opinion/argument.	The conclusion leaves the reader understanding the writer's opinion. Author summarizes opinion/argument.	Author is not clear in summarizing opinion/argument.	There is no conclusion.
Grammar and spelling	Contains few if any errors.	Contains few errors and errors do not interfere with meaning.	Contains many errors and errors interfere with meaning.	Contains many errors that interfere with meaning and make essay illegible.

Persuasive Essay Rubric

Name: _____ Essay topic: _____

| Concerns
Areas for improvement | Criteria for Proficient Work | Advanced
Evidence of exceeding standards |
|---|---|---|
| | **Criteria #1: Focus/topic/opening**
Clearly names the personal opinion. Makes some reference to the main points of the opinion/argument. | |
| | **Criteria #2: Support for position**
Includes three or more reasons for the opinion and each reason is supported by evidence (facts, statistics, examples). | |
| | **Criteria #3: Transitions**
Transitions show how ideas are connected, and some variety of transitions are used. | |
| | **Criteria #4: Closing paragraph**
The conclusion leaves the reader understanding the writer's opinion. Author summarizes opinion/argument. | |
| | **Criteria #5: Grammar and spelling**
Contains few errors and errors do not interfere with meaning. | |

Open-ended questions prompt reflective thinking

Open-ended questions that you ask during coaching and at the end of lessons are a great way to help students synthesize new information, think critically about their work, and identify new directions in learning.

* Questions such as "What are some ways you figured that out?" and "What more would you like to learn about this?" prompt students to think about their own thinking.

* Questions such as "How is this strategy helping you?" or "What about your work is (or is not) the way you wanted it to be?" help students reflect on progress and think about whether they need to change anything in their process.

* Questions such as "What do you know?" "What don't you know yet?" and "What do you want to know?" help students think critically about their learning.

Reflection formats provide structure for students' thinking about their work

You can incorporate reflection into daily instruction through regular use of open-ended questions. You can also provide formats for more structured reflection that students can use anytime to reflect on goals and on work they've done to reach those goals. Following are three tools that help structure reflection.

Reflection sheets. Reflection sheets, which you can use as part of closing a lesson or unit, might include questions and prompts such as:

* What am I learning from this assignment?

* How am I meeting my goal for learning?

F A Q • Where does peer feedback fit?

If managed well, having students give each other feedback on work in progress is valuable and can increase their engagement with learning. Peer feedback works best in partnerships or small groups of three students. Using a checklist or rubric, students listen to or look at classmates' work and provide specific feedback on what is going well and suggestions for improvement. Students incorporate this feedback as they continue their work.

Introduce peer feedback after you've established a positive classroom climate of trust and respect. Take the time to teach, model, and practice the various skills involved, such as how to give and receive both positive and negative feedback.

✳ What do I enjoy about this assignment?

✳ What am I finding hard or challenging about this assignment?

✳ What was the most important thing I learned in doing this activity or assignment?

✳ I am proud of _____.

✳ My goal for next time is _____.

Reflection journals. Students can keep a daily or weekly journal to record reflections on their own learning, challenges, and accomplishments, in response to prompts that you provide. The prompts might include questions and statements similar to those on reflection sheets.

You might also make these prompts specific to a particular assignment, as Ms. Johnson did when she asked students to reflect on one strength in their essay and one thing they wanted to work on.

Online tools. Some teachers use online tools such as blogs or shared documents as a way for students to record their reflections. These can be set up to be private between the student and teacher or shared with the classroom community.

Use Modeling to Introduce Self-Assessment Tools

As with any important and new routine, students need explicit teaching about how to use various self-assessment tools to guide growth. The first step is emphasizing with students that self-assessments are tools that will help them improve skills and grow as learners.

Then you'll need to teach the use of each tool and give students opportunities to practice different parts of the self-assessment process, such as brainstorming criteria for assessment and applying the criteria to their own work. Interactive Modeling (Appendix B) is a useful strategy for teaching these skills and routines.

In the following example, Mr. Lin, the second grade teacher you read about on page 159, uses Interactive Modeling to help students learn how to use a checklist to guide work.

Mr. Lin holds up a checklist of expectations for spelling practice. "You're going to be using checklists like this a lot in school this year. Checklists will help you stay on track and improve as readers, writers, spellers, scientists, and mathematicians. I'm going to demonstrate how to use this checklist and let you hear what I'm thinking. Notice my thoughts as I use the checklist to guide my practice of spelling words."

He pretends to look at a list of spelling words and then look at the checklist.

"Hmm, let's see. I chose the words that I have trouble with. I wrote them from memory and then checked them in the book. I forgot to make a new list of words I need to keep working on."

He asks students what they noticed. They mention that he looked at each item on the list and that he was calm and matter-of-fact. He didn't sound mad at himself for forgetting.

"Yes, that's really important," he said. "The checklists are there to help you learn and grow. I'll be checking in with you this week to see how it's going with using the checklists."

As the weeks go on, Mr. Lin uses reinforcing language to support students' positive efforts with checklists: "Shelby, you used the checklist to help you remember a key step in that math process. You're becoming a mathematician!"

F A Q • Are growth portfolios a form of self-assessment?

Growth portfolios tell the story of a student's efforts, progress, growth, and achievement over time and can certainly be used for self-assessment. In fact, portfolios work best when used for frequent formative self-assessment, not just for work at the end of a unit or school year.

Items shared in a portfolio might include the student's goals for learning, samples of the student's best work, and reflections on how each piece demonstrates progress toward the goals, including checklists and rubrics.

FINAL THOUGHT: STUDENTS BECOME ACTIVE PARTICIPANTS IN LEARNING

As you continue to offer students the teacher assessment and feedback that are central to their growth and learning, we hope you'll incorporate a range of self-assessment opportunities into your daily instruction. Through self-assessment, students begin to recognize for themselves what they know, what they don't know, and what they want to know. They become aware of their own strengths

and challenges and more familiar with their beliefs and misconceptions. And when students know themselves better, their learning deepens. They're more apt to set higher goals for themselves, become more self-motivated, and demonstrate more perseverance toward reaching their goals. In other words, they become engaged learners.

WORKS CITED

Deak, J. (2010). *Your Fantastic Elastic Brain*. San Francisco: Little Pickle Press.

Dweck, C. (2010). *Mindset: The New Psychology of Success*. New York: Ballantine Books.

Teacher Language

A teacher's language is powerful. With your words and tone, you can establish an atmosphere of warmth, safety, and caring and communicate a belief in students' desire and ability to learn. Your language can encourage students to be active learners and to persevere when a task becomes challenging.

Three kinds of teacher language are especially important for building academic engagement:

* **Reinforcing language**

* **Envisioning language**

* **Open-ended questions**

Reinforcing Language Gives Specific, Positive Feedback

When students make choices or exhibit behaviors you want to encourage, giving them positive, honest, and specific feedback builds their self-confidence and lets them know what they are doing well and exactly what actions to keep doing and to build on.

For example, after observing students following established routines for returning books in the classroom library, a teacher might say to the class,

> "Everyone has carefully returned books to our classroom library shelves. This helps us all quickly and easily find the books we are looking for!"

To provide reinforcement to an individual student, the teacher might say to the student privately,

> "I saw you carefully place your book back on the shelf. That's really taking care of our classroom library."

It's important to give individual reinforcement privately. With public recognition, a student might feel embarrassed or uncomfortable for being singled out. Such public recognition might also foster a sense of competition for your attention.

Tips for using reinforcing language effectively

* **Look for and name specific behaviors.** When you give feedback about specific positive aspects of children's behavior or work, you help them become aware of what they know, what they can do, and how they've progressed:

> "Did you notice how many facts we listed about Arctic animals? This class knows a lot about living in this special climate region."

This awareness leads to optimal growth and learning.

* **Emphasize description over personal approval.** When you give your personal approval of children's work and behavior by using phrases like "I love . . ." or "I like how you . . ." you undermine the self-control and intrinsic motivation that children need to develop if they're to be successful learners. When you focus instead on their actions and how those actions support learning goals, you motivate them to act in positive ways for their own sake and the sake of the group. For example, instead of saying "I love your use of a simile here in your story" try:

> "You used a simile here in your story. That helps the reader feel how exciting this race was for the main characters."

* **Name only truly important behaviors.** Instead of offering feedback on every positive action, no matter how small, notice and comment on things that reflect important goals and values. This will ensure that feedback is meaningful and supports children's learning.

For example, if going to the right table to work is a routine that the class has down pat, there's no need to reinforce that behavior. But if working quietly at the table is still at times challenging, then you would want to reinforce that behavior:

> "I noticed you working quietly at your table. It looked like that quietness helped your tablemates concentrate on their writing."

Envisioning Language Inspires Children

Envisioning language inspires children to picture something bigger and brighter than their current reality, gets them excited about that vision, and helps them feel competent to reach it. Specifically, envisioning language names positive identities for children and helps them form a vision of themselves as learners.

For example, in the introduction to a fourth grade science lesson, a teacher might say:

> "Today, you'll get to be scientists studying the properties of light and shadow. Scientists ask questions, observe closely, and try things out."

And before a challenging math lesson, a teacher might say:

> "You are ready to take another step on your learning path. Today you're going to be working on some challenging math problems that I know you can tackle. What are some strategies you might use to help you stick with it and find some solutions to these tricky word problems?"

Tips for crafting effective envisioning statements

Reflect on what matters to children and connect the work of school to these personal motivations. Some ways to make that connection:

✳ **Think about positive identities for children.** Calling students "readers," "writers," "scientists," "athletes," "teammates," "artists," or "musicians" can generate excitement and help students create an identity as successful learners. Draw on your true beliefs about what is possible. For example,

> "You are strong thinkers who are ready to learn!"

* **Use concrete images and words that children use,** rather than abstract terms. One way to do this is to ask children to draw on prior knowledge and then use their words. So before students start drafting personal essays, you might ask them to name what gets their attention when they're reading and brings a story to life. "When you can see things as if you were there," they might say, or "When you feel like you can hear sounds and voices and sort of smell what they're having for dinner." You might then say,

> "Today, you're going to write stories that help readers see, smell, and hear what's going on."

* **Use metaphors to add clarity and power.** Metaphors might come from the curriculum, classroom life, or your own experiences. For example, if you know that children love to build things—the taller, the better—you might use a metaphor of building a tower:

> "Suppose you were building a tower to the sun; you'd need lots of bricks. Math facts are your bricks; when you get good at using them, you can build all sorts of interesting things."

Open-Ended Questions Stretch Children's Thinking

Asking children open-ended questions can stimulate and stretch their curiosity, reasoning ability, creativity, and independence so that they can learn more broadly and deeply.

Open-ended questions have no right or wrong answer

Any reasoned and relevant response to an open-ended question is a good one. Open-ended questions draw on students' own thoughts, knowledge, skills, experiences, and feelings. They encourage students to be inquisitive and to seek answers to satisfy their wonderings. Here are some examples:

"What do you want to try?"

"What might work?"

"What's hard for you?"

"How would you describe the problem?"

"What do you notice about this [poem, painting, math problem]?"

"When have you used [dictionaries, rulers, scooters] before?"

When you ask students such questions, you show trust in their ability to have good ideas, to think for themselves, and to contribute in valuable ways to the class. You help students feel a sense of autonomy, competence, and belonging, and these feelings can lead them to become more engaged in their learning.

When children respond to open-ended questions, they use analysis, synthesis, prediction, comparison, evaluation, and creativity. They make meaning for themselves, which is a key part of active learning.

Open-ended questions help children build on their knowledge

Open-ended questions can help you learn what children know or understand about a topic or process. When you start with what children already know and are ready to learn next and then help them build from there, they're more likely to take learning risks, support each other's explorations, and succeed with their work—all of which makes learning more meaningful and interesting.

Open-ended questions work well in many situations

You can use open-ended questions in many classroom situations, including when introducing a lesson or activity, when coaching children as they work on a project or task, when solving problems, and at the close of a lesson or activity. You can also use these questions for a variety of purposes, such as to increase children's awareness of what they already know, to generate interest or ideas, to help students plan, or to promote reflection.

Tips for asking effective open-ended questions

✳ **Be truly curious.** For open-ended questions to be effective, it's important to ask them with genuine curiosity about students' thinking processes, with as much focus on how they arrived at their answers as on the answers themselves. For example:

> "What are some ways you figured this out?"

> "What part of this do you find most interesting?"

✳ **Clarify exactly what you are asking for.** To stimulate on-topic responses, provide students with boundaries for what you want them to think about. For example, instead of asking a general question, like "How could you use the globe?" you might ask,

> "How could you use the globe to discover facts about continents?"

✳ **Use words that encourage cooperation, not competition.** When you ask questions such as "Who has a better idea?" students might feel competitive and assume some answers are valued more than others. Instead, to encourage cooperation and sharing of ideas you could ask,

> "Who has a different idea?"

To learn about other kinds of positive teacher language, see *The Power of Our Words: Teacher Language That Helps Children Learn*, 2nd ed., by Paula Denton, EdD, Center for Responsive Schools, Inc., 2014.

Interactive Modeling

Interactive Modeling is a simple and extremely effective way to engage students in actively learning a routine or skill that needs to be done in one specific way. Unlike conventional modeling, which focuses primarily on what you're doing, Interactive Modeling involves students as active participants throughout the process. They're challenged to watch a demonstration, notice the details for themselves, and then name those details out loud; they then gain immediate experience by practicing the routine or skill right away, while you coach and give feedback on their efforts.

The seven steps of Interactive Modeling might take ten or fifteen minutes—a small investment of time that will help you spend more time teaching and students spend more time learning. Students will ask fewer questions about procedures and directions, require less time for cleaning up, and find and care for materials more easily and independently. And because they have taken part in the modeling, students will be more motivated to follow the modeled procedure and will tend to remember more of what they've learned.

Seven Steps of Interactive Modeling

1. Say what you will model and why.

2. Model the behavior.

3. Ask students what they noticed.

4. Invite one or more students to model.

5. Again, ask students what they noticed.

6. Have all students practice.

7. Provide feedback.

Use Interactive Modeling to Teach a Variety of Skills

Interactive Modeling works for students of all ages and for teachers in any role, including special area teachers, teachers of special education, administrators, and coaches.

You can use Interactive Modeling to teach a range of skills that are key to increasing students' academic engagement. For example, before children look up information on the Internet for a research project, you might use Interactive Modeling to teach them how to do a focused search and how to choose reliable sources.

Or when you want children to work with partners to read and report on a piece of text, you can first use Interactive Modeling to teach careful and respectful listening.

Skills and Routines to Teach With Interactive Modeling

➤ Using the classroom library (taking books off the shelf, using them carefully, putting them back in the right place)

➤ Doing classroom routines (responding to the signal for quiet, choosing where in the circle to sit)

➤ Doing academic activities (giving peer feedback, adding ideas to a Venn diagram, reading with a partner, conducting an interview)

➤ Working with a partner (speaking and listening respectfully, taking turns, making a choice together, reading together, sharing materials)

➤ Taking part in a discussion (asking clarifying questions, backing up an assertion with evidence, expressing disagreement honestly but respectfully)

➤ Using the computer (creating, saving, and organizing files; bookmarking a website; accessing material on Blackboard)

➤ Using print resources (dictionary, atlas, magazines and journals)

➤ Doing activities in PE or at recess (performing a sit-up or push-up, tagging safely, using a scooter safely, gathering and stacking marker cones)

➤ Doing activities in music class (counting beats in a song, playing and caring for specific musical instruments)

➤ Using and caring for common supplies (organizing notebooks or folders, mixing paint, measuring with a ruler, putting tops on markers, using glue sticks, sharpening pencils, looking through a hand lens, washing and storing paint-brushes, storing modeling clay)

Use Interactive Modeling Throughout the Year

Interactive Modeling is especially useful at the beginning of the school year, when you're establishing expectations and helping students learn new skills and routines. Although you may feel pressure to start right in with academic content, taking the time to teach the necessary skills and routines that rigorous academic work requires helps draw students in, increases their attentiveness, and deepens their involvement with their learning.

However, you don't need to model and practice every new routine and skill right away. Focus on the ones that are essential for current learning tasks, are more complex than usual, or are likely to be used frequently in coming months.

Then, throughout the year you can continue to use Interactive Modeling to teach new skills—and reteach previously learned ones if things start to get a bit ragged. When reteaching skills and routines you might just use an abbreviated format; for example, you could skip steps 2 and 3 (teacher modeling and asking students what they notice) and go straight to step 4 (student volunteers doing the modeling).

Interactive Modeling in Action

Following are four examples of Interactive Modeling at a range of grade levels to give you an idea of what this strategy looks and sounds like in action. You will also find examples of Interactive Modeling in action throughout this book. To learn more, see *Interactive Modeling: A Powerful Technique for Teaching Children* by Margaret Berry Wilson, Center for Responsive Schools, Inc., 2012.

How to wash and store paintbrushes

GRADES K – 1

15 minutes

Steps	What It Might Sound/Look Like
1. Say what you will model and why.	"If we want our supplies to last, we need to take care of them. I want to show you how to clean the paintbrushes so that they'll last a long time and we'll always have them available for all the art we'll be creating. Watch me carefully and see what you notice."
2. Model the behavior.	Have a paintbrush sitting in a small container of paint at a table and sit at the table as though you just finished painting. Without narrating what you're doing (narrating distracts students from noticing your actions), stand up, push in your chair or stool, then pick up the brush in one hand and wipe off excess paint on the edges of the container. Holding one hand under the tip of the paintbrush to catch any drips, walk slowly to the sink and turn on the water to a medium flow. Hold the tip of the paintbrush under the water, using your other hand to gently massage the tip of the brush to get all the paint out. Turn off the water and place the paintbrush in the holder next to the sink with the brush tip pointing up. Take a paper towel and dry off your hands. Then use the same paper towel to wipe around the edge of the sink, and put the towel in the trashcan.

3. Ask students what they noticed.	"What did you notice about what I did to clean the paintbrush?" If necessary, prompt students to recall the details you want to be sure they learn: "What did I do at the table before I walked to the sink?" "How did I get the paintbrush clean?" "Where does the paintbrush go to dry?" "What did I do with the paper towel?"
4. Invite one or more students to model.	"Who can show us how to clean a paintbrush the same way I did?"
5. Again, ask students what they noticed.	"What did you notice about the way Jayden cleaned his paintbrush?"
6. Have all students practice.	"During art class today, you're going to create a painting, and then you can all practice cleaning your paintbrushes. I'll be watching and seeing you do all the things we just noticed."
7. Provide feedback.	Use reinforcing language (see Appendix A) to give feedback. To the whole group: "I saw everyone carrying the paintbrushes carefully as you moved from the tables to the sink. The paintbrushes look clean and the brush ends are all pointing up so they can dry. And the sink area looks clean and dry. Looks like our paintbrushes will last for a very long time." Privately, to an individual: "You took time to wipe down the sink after rinsing your paintbrush. That helps keep our work areas clean."

Steps	What It Might Sound/Look Like
1. Say what you will model and why.	"Sometimes in our class you'll have opportunities to read with a partner. Later in the year we'll talk about how you and your partner can decide who will read first, but for now, the person whose first initial comes first in the alphabet gets to read first. "We need to be respectful of our reading partners and share materials so we can all do our best learning. Mr. Gomez and I are going to show you what partner reading looks like and sounds like in this class. Watch what we do."
2. Model the behavior.	Sit next to your partner, either on chairs or on the floor. Have one book to share. "Hi, Mr. Gomez. This is the book we are going to read together." Hand the book to Mr. Gomez. "Your initial comes before mine in the alphabet so you read first." "OK. Should we take turns reading each page or each section of the book?" Take turns reading, with the reader holding the book in such a way that the partner can also look on. Carefully pass the book when it's time for the partner to begin reading.
3. Ask students what they noticed.	"What did you notice about our partner reading?" If necessary, prompt students to recall the details you want to be sure they learn, asking questions such as "What did we say or do before we started reading?" "What did you notice about how each partner was holding the book?" "What did our voices sound like as we were taking turns to read?"

4. Invite one or more students to model.	"Let's see if we have two volunteers who can partner read a book the same way we just did."
5. Again, ask students what they noticed.	"What did you notice about what Gianna and Isaiah did to read a book together?"
6. Have all students practice.	"Now we're all going to have a chance to practice reading with a partner. Today, for practice, I have some familiar picture books for you to read. Your partner is listed here on the board. Find a spot in the room to sit with each other and I will bring you a book."
7. Provide feedback.	After five to seven minutes of reading, signal for quiet attention, even if some partners are not finished reading. Use reinforcing language (see Appendix A) to give feedback. To the whole group: "I noticed that you all talked with your partners before you got started to figure out how to read the book and to identify who would go first. I saw students passing the book carefully back and forth, and partners looking on as others read aloud in a clear but quiet voice. Looks like we are ready to do more reading with each other in this classroom." To an individual student, privately: "Geneen, you read aloud with a clear but quiet voice so that Tim could hear you but you didn't disturb other pairs."

How to measure accurately with a ruler

10–15 minutes

Steps	What It Might Sound/Look Like
1. Say what you will model and why.	"When we measure with a ruler, it's important to do it accurately and precisely. I'm going to show you how to do that by measuring the length of this book. Watch and see what you notice."
2. Model the behavior.	Without talking, carefully line up the zero mark at one end of the book. Make sure the ruler is straight across the book and carefully note the ending spot. Announce the measurement to the class: "Fifteen and a half centimeters."
3. Ask students what they noticed.	"What did you notice about how I tried to be accurate as I measured?"
	If necessary, prompt students to recall the details you want to be sure they learn, asking questions such as "How did I place the ruler?" "How did I line the ruler up with the edge of the book?" "What did you notice me doing on this end to make sure my measurement was correct?"
4. Invite one or more students to model.	"Who can show us how to measure another book the same way I did?"
5. Again, ask students what they noticed.	"What did you notice Ramon doing to make sure his measurement was accurate?"
6. Have all students practice.	"Now we're all going to practice measuring a list of objects in the room. I'll be watching to see how precisely and accurately you use the ruler."

7. Provide feedback.

Use reinforcing language (see Appendix A) to give feedback.

To the whole group: "You were all being careful to line up your ruler on zero and hold the ruler straight. That will help you get accurate measurements."

To an individual student, privately: "I noticed you lined up the ruler on zero and were very exact at the end. That's what it takes for careful, accurate measuring."

How to give feedback on someone's work

GRADES 4 – 6

Steps	What It Might Sound/Look Like
1. Say what you will model and why.	"In our class, you'll have opportunities to share your work with each other and give each other feedback. When we give a classmate feedback on their work, it's important to be honest, specific, and respectful. We want to take care of each other as we comment." "I'm going to use this science poster about volcanoes that a student created last year to demonstrate how to give honest, specific, respectful feedback about a classmate's work. Notice what I do."
2. Model the behavior.	Give everyone a minute to look over the poster. Then say (pretending to speak to a student who created the poster), "Your poster is bright and easy to read. The diagram of the volcano is clearly labeled with words and color. Everything is glued down securely. I learned a lot about volcanoes from reading the facts you included on your poster. You say how many volcanoes there are around the world. But I wonder how many active volcanoes there are? Are there any in the United States?"
3. Ask students what they noticed.	"What did you notice about the way I gave feedback?" If necessary, prompt students to recall the details you want to be sure they learn, asking questions such as "How did I take care of this student while I gave feedback?" "In what ways were my comments specific? Honest?" "What was the tone of my voice like?"

4. Invite one or more students to model.	"When we give feedback, we want to be honest, specific, and respectful. We want to focus on the positive and if we do have a suggestion, we want to state it carefully so our classmate feels positive about their work. Who wants to try doing those things with another poster created by a student last year?"
5. Again, ask students what they noticed.	"What did you notice that Tariq did to be specific, honest, and respectful and to make a helpful suggestion?"
6. Have all students practice.	Share one more piece of work with students. Pair students up and coach them in giving feedback about the sample work.
7. Provide feedback.	Use reinforcing language (Appendix A) to give feedback.

To the whole group: "I hear positive and respectful comments. I hear encouraging statements. Your feedback will help this student improve his work."

To an individual student, privately: "Sounds like you were taking care of the student who created this work by keeping your comments positive and encouraging. And your suggestion was stated respectfully. Comments like these will help students learn and improve their work." |

Planning Guides

In this appendix you'll find the following:

✳ **Interactive Modeling Planning Guide**

✳ **Guided Discovery Planning Guide**

✳ **Role-Play Planning Guide**

✳ **Lesson Planning Guide**

✳ **Academic Choice Planning Guide**

Each guide includes questions to prompt your thinking. Feel free to photocopy these guides for repeated use. You can also download and print PDFs of these guides from our website—just go to *The Joyful Classroom* product page in our online bookstore, where you'll find a link to the PDFs: www.responsiveclassroom.org/store/.

Interactive Modeling Planning Guide

Steps	What I Plan to Say/Do
1. Say what you will model and why.	What one or two positively stated sentences will you say?
2. Model the behavior.	What will you do to show the expected, positive behavior?
3. Ask students what they noticed.	What questions will you ask? What do you want to be sure children understand about how to do the behavior?

4. Invite one or more students to model.	How will you set this up? What will you say?
5. Again, ask students what they noticed.	What questions will you ask? What do you want to be sure children understand about how to do the behavior?
6. Have all students practice.	What will you have them do? How will you set this up?
7. Provide feedback.	What will you reinforce? What are some words you can use? What tone of voice will you use?

Guided Discovery Planning Guide

Steps	What I Plan to Say/Do
1. Introduction and naming	What material are you introducing? If introducing a familiar material, how will you get children to look at it in a new way and notice new things? What open-ended questions can you ask? What vocabulary do you want to emphasize or introduce?
2. Generation and modeling of students' ideas for use and care of material	How will you help children generate ideas and model behaviors needed for careful, learning-focused use of the material during the exploration step coming up?

3. Exploration	How will you facilitate children's exploration of the material? Where will the exploration happen? What behaviors do you want to reinforce?
4. Sharing exploratory work	How will you facilitate children's sharing of their work and ideas? What focus will you provide?
5. Cleanup and care of material	How will you help children think through and practice cleanup and care of material? What do children need to know? What behaviors will you model?

Role-Play Planning Guide

Steps	What I Plan to Say/Do
1. Describe a specific situation. Stop at the point where a behavior decision will occur.	What situation will the class role-play? How will you describe the situation from a student's point of view? How will you connect to classroom rules? At what point will you stop?
2. Name the positive goal.	What goal do you want the children to meet as they decide how to behave in this situation? How will you convey this goal? For example: "How can I give constructive feedback in a kind, respectful way?"
3. Invite and record students' ideas for a solution.	How will you invite ideas? How many ideas will you record? How will you redirect any inappropriate ideas?
4. Act out one idea with the teacher in the lead—or "tricky"— role. Audience notices what actors say and do.	Who will you choose to act out other roles? Where will you stop the action so that the role-play stays positive?
5. Ask students what they noticed.	What questions can you ask to elicit specific observations? For example: "What did you notice about the way . . . ?" "What did it feel like to . . . ?" "How was this an example of following our rules?"

6. Act out another idea; consider having a student take the lead role. Audience notices what actors say and do.	Are students ready to take the lead role? If so, who will take the lead role? Who will act out other roles? Where will you stop the action so that the role-play stays positive?
7. Again, ask students what they noticed.	For example: "What did you notice about the way . . . ?" "What did it feel like to . . . ?" "How was this an example of following our rules?"
8. Act out other ideas.	Assess focus and energy. Is the class ready to act out other ideas? If so, who will take the roles?
9. Sum up lessons learned.	What points do you want to emphasize? What do you want students to remember?
10. Follow up.	How and when will you follow up on this role-play?

Lesson Planning Guide

Topic/unit of study _____

Goal/purpose _____

CCSS/curriculum standard _____

Time needed: _____

Preparation: What materials do you need? Do you need to introduce any materials using Guided Discovery? Do you need to use Interactive Modeling to teach how to use any of the materials?

Are there any skills or routines you need to teach using Interactive Modeling?

Opening (_____ minutes) **Elements of engagement to include in the opening:** ❏ ILS ❏ Things kids love to do ❏ Partners/small groups ❏ Choices	How will you share the purpose of the lesson in student-friendly language? What connections can you make to students' interests and strengths? What activities will students do?

Body (_____ minutes) **Elements of engagement to include in the body:** ❑ ILS ❑ Things kids love to do ❑ Partners/small groups ❑ Choices	How will students work with the content of the lesson? For example, what are their tasks, how will they be grouped, what interactive learning structures will you use, and will you offer them choices? What skills do students need for this work? How will you model these skills for them?
Closing (_____ minutes) **Elements of engagement to include in the closing:** ❑ ILS ❑ Things kids love to do ❑ Partners/small groups ❑ Choices ❑ Student self-assessment	How can the lesson be summarized and connected to other learning? How can students reflect on their learning? How might they share reflections with others?

Academic Choice Planning Guide

Topic/unit of study:

Goal:

"What" Choice: (Will you offer "what" choices? If so, which ones will you need to demonstrate or review?)	"How" Choice: (Will you offer "how" choices? If so, which ones will you need to demonstrate or review?)

Plan: Will you have students sign up orally? Sign up on the board? Complete a planning sheet? How can you help students make a "good-fit" choice?

Work: Where will students work? (Assigned places or student choice?) With whom will they work? (Individually, partners, small groups? Teacher-assigned or student choice?) How will you coach students?

Reflect: How will students reflect? (Privately? With a partner? With the whole group?) What might you name as a focus for reflection?

Notes:

All of the recommended practices in this book come from or are consistent with the *Responsive Classroom* approach to teaching—a research-based education approach associated with greater teacher effectiveness, higher student achievement, and improved school climate. *Responsive Classroom* practices help educators build competencies in four interrelated domains: engaging academics, positive community, effective management, and developmentally responsive teaching.

To learn more about the *Responsive Classroom* approach, see the following resources published by Center for Responsive Schools and available from www.responsiveclassroom.org • 800-360-6332.

Classroom Management: Set up and run a classroom in ways that enable the best possible teaching and learning.

> *Interactive Modeling: A Powerful Technique for Teaching Children* by Margaret Berry Wilson. 2012.

> *What Every Teacher Needs to Know*, K–5 series, by Margaret Berry Wilson and Mike Anderson. 2010–2011.

> *Teaching Children to Care: Classroom Management for Ethical and Academic Growth K–8*, revised ed., by Ruth Sidney Charney. 2002.

Morning Meeting: Gather as a whole class each morning to greet each other, share news, and warm up for the day of learning ahead.

> *The Morning Meeting Book*, 3rd ed., by Roxann Kriete and Carol Davis. 2014.

> *80 Morning Meeting Ideas for Grades K–2* by Susan Lattanzi Roser. 2012.

> *80 Morning Meeting Ideas for Grades 3–6* by Carol Davis. 2012.

Doing Language Arts in Morning Meeting: 150 Quick Activities That Connect to Your Curriculum by Jodie Luongo, Joan Riordan, and Kate Umstatter. 2015. (Includes a Common Core State Standards correlation guide.)

Doing Math in Morning Meeting: 150 Quick Activities That Connect to Your Curriculum by Andy Dousis and Margaret Berry Wilson. 2010. (Includes a Common Core State Standards correlation guide.)

Doing Science in Morning Meeting: 150 Quick Activities That Connect to Your Curriculum by Lara Webb and Margaret Berry Wilson. 2013. (Includes correlation guides to the Next Generation Science Standards and *A Framework for K–12 Science Education*, the basis for the standards.)

Morning Meeting Professional Development Kit. 2008.

Positive Teacher Language: Use words and tone as a tool to promote students' active learning, sense of community, and self-discipline.

The Power of Our Words: Teacher Language That Helps Children Learn, 2nd ed., by Paula Denton, EdD. 2014.

Teacher Language for Engaged Learning: 4 Video Study Sessions. 2013.

Teacher Language Professional Development Kit. 2010.

Engaging Academics: Learn tools for effective teaching and making lessons lively, appropriately challenging, and purposeful to help students develop higher levels of motivation, persistence, and mastery of skills and content.

The Language of Learning: Teaching Students Core Thinking, Speaking, and Listening Skills by Margaret Berry Wilson. 2014.

Teaching Discipline: Use practical strategies, such as rule creation and positive responses to misbehavior, to promote self-discipline in students and build a safe, calm, and respectful school climate.

Teasing, Tattling, Defiance and More: Positive Approaches to 10 Common Classroom Behaviors by Margaret Berry Wilson. 2013.

Rules in School: Teaching Discipline in the Responsive Classroom, 2nd ed., by Kathryn Brady, Mary Beth Forton, and Deborah Porter. 2011.

Responsive School Discipline: Essentials for Elementary School Leaders by Chip Wood and Babs Freeman-Loftis. 2011.

Teaching Discipline in the Classroom Professional Development Kit. 2011.

Foundation-Setting During the First Weeks of School: Take time in the critical first weeks of school to establish expectations, routines, a sense of community, and a positive classroom tone.

The First Six Weeks of School, 2nd ed. From *Responsive Classroom*. 2015.

Movement, Games, Songs, and Chants: Sprinkle quick, lively activities throughout the school day to keep students energized, engaged, and alert.

Closing Circles: 50 Activities for Ending the Day in a Positive Way by Dana Januszka and Kristen Vincent. 2012.

Energizers! 88 Quick Movement Activities That Refresh and Refocus by Susan Lattanzi Roser. 2009.

99 Activities and Greetings: Great for Morning Meeting … and other meetings, too! by Melissa Correa-Connolly. 2004.

Preventing Bullying at School: Use practical strategies throughout the day to create a safe, kind environment in which bullying is far less likely to take root.

How to Bullyproof Your Classroom by Caltha Crowe. 2012. (Includes bullying prevention lessons.)

Solving Behavior Problems With Children: Engage students in solving their behavior problems so they feel safe, challenged, and invested in changing.

Sammy and His Behavior Problems: Stories and Strategies from a Teacher's Year by Caltha Crowe. 2010.

Solving Thorny Behavior Problems: How Teachers and Students Can Work Together by Caltha Crowe. 2009.

Child Development: Understand children's common physical, social-emotional, cognitive, and language characteristics at each age, and adapt teaching to respond to children's developmental needs.

Yardsticks: Children in the Classroom Ages 4–14, 3rd ed., by Chip Wood. 2007.

Child Development Pamphlet Series, K–8 (based on *Yardsticks* by Chip Wood; available in English and Spanish). 2005 and 2006.

***Responsive Classroom* for Special Area Educators:** Explore key *Responsive Classroom* practices adapted for a wide variety of special areas.

Responsive Classroom for Music, Art, PE, and Other Special Areas. From *Responsive Classroom.* August 2016.

Working With Families: Hear parents' insights, help them understand the school's teaching approaches, and engage them as partners in their children's education.

Parents & Teachers Working Together by Carol Davis and Alice Yang. 2005.

Professional Development/Staff Meetings: Learn easy-to-use structures for getting the most out of your work with colleagues.

Energize Your Meetings! 35 Interactive Learning Structures for Educators. From *Responsive Classroom.* 2014.

INDEX

About the Publisher

Center for Responsive Schools, Inc., a not-for-profit educational organization, is the developer of *Responsive Classroom®*, a research-based education approach associated with greater teacher effectiveness, higher student achievement, and improved school climate. *Responsive Classroom* practices help educators build competencies in four interrelated domains: engaging academics, positive community, effective management, and developmentally responsive teaching. We offer the following resources for educators:

PROFESSIONAL DEVELOPMENT SERVICES

➤ Workshops for K–8 educators (locations around the country and internationally)

➤ On-site consulting services to support implementation

➤ Resources for site-based study

➤ Annual conferences for K–8 educators

PUBLICATIONS AND RESOURCES

➤ Books and videos

➤ Professional development kits for school-based study

➤ Free monthly newsletter

➤ Extensive library of free articles on our website

FOR DETAILS, CONTACT:

Responsive Classroom®

Center for Responsive Schools, Inc.
85 Avenue A, P.O. Box 718
Turners Falls, Massachusetts 01376-0718

800-360-6332   www.responsiveclassroom.org
info@responsiveclassroom.org